GRADE
6

STAAR Mathematics

PRACTICE

T5-BAW-242

Table of Contents

Using This Book

What Is the STAAR Mathematics Assessment?

The State of Texas Assessments of Academic Readiness (STAAR) is the current assessment for students in the state of Texas. STAAR Mathematics assesses what students are expected to learn at each grade level according to the developmentally appropriate academic readiness and supporting standards outlined in the Texas Essential Knowledge and Skills (TEKS).

How Does This Book Help My Student(s)?

If your student is taking the STAAR Assessment for Mathematics, then as a teacher and/or parent you can use the mini-lessons, math practice pages and practice tests in this book to prepare for the STAAR Mathematics exam. This book is appropriate for on-grade-level students.

STAAR Mathematics Practice provides:

- Mini-lessons for assessed Math TEKS skills and strategies
- Word problems for assessed Math TEKS skills and strategies
- Questions for griddable and multiple-choice answer format
- Opportunities to familiarize students with STAAR format and question stems

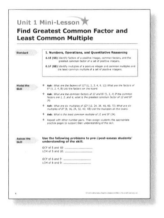

Introduce STAAR-aligned math concept, skill, or strategy

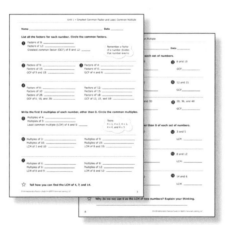

Practice with STAAR-aligned problems

Assess concepts, skills, and strategies with word problems

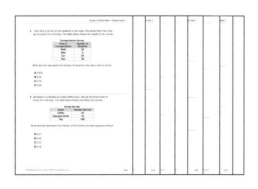

Simulate test-taking with full-length practice tests

STAAR Mathematics Practice/Assessed TEKS Alignment Chart • Grade 6

I. Number, Operations, and Quantitative Reasoning	6.1	6.2	6.3	6.4	6.5	6.6	6.7	6.8	6.9	6.10	6.11–6.13
Unit 1: Find Greatest Common Factor and Least Common Multiple	✔										✔
Unit 2: Write Prime Factorizations	✔										✔
Unit 3: Understand Integers	✔										✔
Unit 4: Use Order of Operations		✔									✔
Unit 5: Estimate		✔									✔
Unit 6: Divide Multi-Digit Whole Numbers		✔									✔
Unit 7: Add and Subtract Decimals		✔									✔
Unit 8: Generate Equivalent Forms of Rational Numbers	✔										✔
Unit 9: Compare and Order Rational Numbers	✔										✔
Unit 10: Add Fractions		✔									✔
Unit 11: Subtract Fractions		✔									✔

II. Patterns, Relationships, and Algebraic Reasoning	6.1	6.2	6.3	6.4	6.5	6.6	6.7	6.8	6.9	6.10	6.11–6.13
Unit 12: Use Ratios and Equivalent Ratios		✔	✔								✔
Unit 13: Use Rates		✔	✔								✔
Unit 14: Understand Percentages			✔								✔
Unit 15: Represent Relationships				✔							✔
Unit 16: Generate Formulas				✔							✔
Unit 17: Write Equations					✔						✔

III. Geometry and Spatial Reasoning	6.1	6.2	6.3	6.4	6.5	6.6	6.7	6.8	6.9	6.10	6.11–6.13
Unit 18: Classify Triangles						✔					✔
Unit 19: Quadrilaterals						✔					✔
Unit 20: Circles						✔					✔
Unit 21: Locate Points on the Coordinate Plane							✔				✔

IV. Measurement	6.1	6.2	6.3	6.4	6.5	6.6	6.7	6.8	6.9	6.10	6.11–6.13
Unit 22: Measure Angles								✔			✔
Unit 23: Convert Measures								✔			✔
Unit 24: Solve Problems Involving Measurements								✔			✔
Unit 25: Estimate Perimeter and Circumference								✔			✔
Unit 26: Estimate and Find Area								✔			✔
Unit 27: Estimate and Find Volume								✔			✔

V. Probability and Statistics	6.1	6.2	6.3	6.4	6.5	6.6	6.7	6.8	6.9	6.10	6.11–6.13
Unit 28: Use Lists and Tree Diagrams									✔		✔
Unit 29: Find Probability									✔		✔
Unit 30: Find Mean, Median, and Mode										✔	✔
Unit 31: Make and Interpret Dot Plots										✔	✔
Unit 32: Make and Interpret Stem and Leaf Plots										✔	✔
Unit 33: Display and Interpret Data										✔	✔
Unit 34: Display Data in Circle Graphs										✔	✔

Unit 1 Mini-Lesson

Find Greatest Common Factor and Least Common Multiple

Standard

> ## I. Number, Operations, and Quantitative Reasoning
>
> **6.1E (SS)** Identify factors of a positive integer, common factors, and the greatest common factor of a set of positive integers.
>
> **6.1F (SS)** Identify multiples of a positive integer and common multiples and the least common multiple of a set of positive integers.

Model the Skill

◆ **Ask:** *What are the factors of 12?* (1, 2, 3, 4, 6, 12) *What are the factors of 8?* (1, 2, 4, 8) List the factors on the board.

◆ **Ask:** *What are the common factors of 12 and 8?* (1, 2, 4) *If the common factors are 1, 2, and 4, what is the greatest common factor of 12 and 8?* (4)

◆ **Ask:** *What are six multiples of 12?* (12, 24, 36, 48, 60, 72) *What are six multiples of 8?* (8, 16, 24, 32, 40, 48) List the multiples on the board.

◆ **Ask:** *What is the least common multiple of 12 and 8?* (24)

◆ Repeat with other number pairs. Then assign students the appropriate practice page(s) to support their understanding of the skill.

Assess the Skill

Use the following problems to pre-/post-assess students' understanding of the skill.

GCF of 5 and 10: _____

LCM of 5 and 10: _____

GCF of 6 and 9: _____

LCM of 6 and 9: _____

STAAR Mathematics Practice Grade 6 • ©2013 Newmark Learning, LLC

Name _____ **Date** _____

List all the factors for each number. Circle the common factors.

1 Factors of 9: _____
Factors of 12: _____
Greatest common factor (GCF) of 9 and 12: _____

> Remember, a factor of a number divides that number evenly.

2 Factors of 9: _____
Factors of 15: _____
GCF of 9 and 15: _____

3 Factors of 4: _____
Factors of 6: _____
GCF of 4 and 6: _____

4 Factors of 6: _____
Factors of 10: _____
Factors of 28: _____
GCF of 6, 10, and 28: _____

5 Factors of 12: _____
Factors of 15: _____
Factors of 18: _____
GCF of 12, 15, and 18: _____

Write the first 5 multiples of each number, other than 0. Circle the common multiples.

6 Multiples of 4: _____
Multiples of 5: _____
Least common multiple (LCM) of 4 and 5: _____

> Think:
> 4 x 1, 4 x 2, 4 x 3, 4 x 4, and 4 x 5

7 Multiples of 4: _____
Multiples of 10: _____
LCM of 4 and 10: _____

8 Multiples of 9: _____
Multiples of 15: _____
LCM of 9 and 15: _____

9 Multiples of 6: _____
Multiples of 9: _____
LCM of 6 and 9: _____

10 Multiples of 8: _____
Multiples of 12: _____
LCM of 8 and 12: _____

 Tell how you can find the LCM of 4, 7, and 14.

Name _____ Date _____

Find the greatest common factor (GCF) of each set of numbers.

1 10 and 25

GCF: _____

2 12 and 8

GCF: _____

3 6 and 15

GCF: _____

4 24 and 60

GCF: _____

5 16 and 6

GCF: _____

6 12 and 21

GCF: _____

7 10 and 30

GCF: _____

8 16, 18, and 30

GCF: _____

9 20, 36, and 48

GCF: _____

Find the least common multiple (LCM) other than 0 of each set of numbers.

10 7 and 9

LCM: _____

11 4 and 10

LCM: _____

12 3 and 5

LCM: _____

13 4 and 6

LCM: _____

14 9 and 6

LCM: _____

15 8 and 12

LCM: _____

16 8 and 3

LCM: _____

17 3 and 23

LCM: _____

18 14 and 6

LCM: _____

☆ **Why do we not use 0 as the LCM of two numbers? Explain your thinking.**

_____

STAAR Mathematics Practice Grade 6 • ©2013 Newmark Learning, LLC

Name _____ **Date** _____

Solve.

1 Dan rides his bike to town every eighth day. Soo walks to town every third day. On which days are they likely to meet in town?

2 $\frac{32}{96}$ of the parents in the PTA wanted a bake sale instead of a car wash. What is the greatest common factor that you could use to simplify this fraction?

3 The ratio of students with bikes to students with scooters in the school is 85:51. What is the greatest common factor that you could use to simplify this ratio?

4 The biology class has a lab every 4 days. The earth science class has a lab every 3 days. On which day do both classes have lab?

5 What is the greatest common factor of 63 and 21?

6 What is the least common multiple of 7 and 12?

Circle the letter for the correct answer.

7 Twenty-eight girls and 35 boys signed up for the team challenge. Each team needs to have an equal number of girls and boys. What is the greatest number of teams possible?

    A 31

    B 14

    C 7

    D 5

8 Every 10 years the alumni have a reunion. Every 2 years the alumni have a soccer game. How often do the reunion and the game fall in the same year?

    A Once every 10 years

    B 5 times every 10 years

    C 20 times every 10 years

    D None of the above

Unit 2 Mini-Lesson ★
Write Prime Factorizations

Standard	**I. Number, Operations, and Quantitative Reasoning** **6.1D (SS)** Write prime factorizations using exponents.

Model the Skill

◆ **Ask:** *What do you remember about prime and composite numbers?* Remind students that a prime number is a whole number greater than 1 and has only two factors, itself and 1. A composite number is a whole number with more than two factors.

◆ **Say:** *Every composite number can be written as the product of two or more prime numbers. We call this product prime factorization.* Demonstrate how to find the prime factorization of 8 with a tree diagram by repeatedly dividing until the factors are prime: 2 x 2 x 2.

◆ **Ask:** *How can we write 2 x 2 x 2 as an exponent?* (2^3) Review how to write an exponent. Have students identify the base and the number of times the base is used as a factor. Continue making factor trees for numbers and finding prime factorization until students understand the process.

◆ Assign students the appropriate practice page(s) to support their understanding of the skill.

Assess the Skill

Use the following problems to pre-/post-assess students' understanding of the skill.

Write the prime factorization for each, using exponents.

16   18   50   28   81   32

Name _____ Date _____

List all the factors for each number. Tell if the number is prime or composite.

1 6

Factors: _____

6 is _____

2 37

Factors: _____

37 is _____

3 63

Factors: _____

63 is _____

4 28

Factors: _____

28 is _____

5 42

Factors: _____

42 is _____

6 31

Factors: _____

31 is _____

Complete each factor tree to show the number as a product of prime factors. Write each prime factorization using exponents.

7
            24
        6 x _____
    3 x _____ x _____ x _____
    prime factorization is _____

8
            12
        2 x _____
    2 x _____ x _____
    prime factorization is _____

9

            40
        _____ x _____
    _____ x _____ x _____
_____ x _____ x _____ x _____
    prime factorization is _____

10

            27
        _____ x _____
    _____ x _____ x _____
    prime factorization is _____

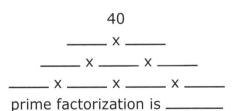 **Tell how you know if a number is a composite number.**

Name _____ **Date** _____

Use a factor tree to find the prime factors for each number. Write the prime factorization using exponents.

❶   28

_____ x _____

_____ x _____ x _____

_____ x _____ x _____ x _____

prime factorization is _____

❷   54

_____ x _____

_____ x _____ x _____

_____ x _____ x _____ x _____

prime factorization is _____

❸   45

prime factorization is _____

❹   20

prime factorization is _____

❺   18

prime factorization is _____

❻   48

prime factorization is _____

❼   72

prime factorization is _____

❽   64

prime factorization is _____

❾   50

prime factorization is _____

❿   125

prime factorization is _____

   Tell how you find the prime factorization of 125.

Name _____ **Date** _____

Solve.

1 Is 109 a prime or a composite number? Explain how you know.

2 What is the prime factorization of 84?

3 What is the prime factorization of 62?

4 What is the prime factorization of 100?

5 What are the two prime factors in the prime factorization of 51? Explain how you know.

6 What is the exponent needed to complete the prime factorization of 63?

$7 \times 3^?$

Circle the letter for the correct answer.

7 What number is shown by the prime factorization $2^2 \times 3^2$?

A 10

B 12

C 24

D 36

8 Which expression shows the prime factorization of 72?

A 3^4

B $3^2 \times 2^2$

C $2^3 \times 3^2$

D $3^3 \times 2^2$

Unit 3 Mini-Lesson ★
Understand Integers

Standard

I. Number, Operations, and Quantitative Reasoning

6.1C (SS) Use integers to represent real-life situations.

Model the Skill

◆ Draw the following number line on the board.

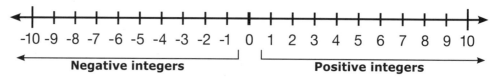

-10 -9 -8 -7 -6 -5 -4 -3 -2 -1 0 1 2 3 4 5 6 7 8 9 10

Negative integers   **Positive integers**

◆ **Say:** *Today we are going to be working with positive and negative integers. Which point on the number line represents negative 6? How do you know? Which point on the number line represents positive 3? How do you know?*

◆ **Say:** *The opposite of an integer is its positive or negative counterpart on the opposite side of the number line. So, whatever lies the exact distance from zero on the other side of the number line is an integer's opposite. The absolute value of an integer is the distance of a number on the number line from 0, no matter which direction from zero the number lies. The absolute value of a number is never negative.*

◆ **Ask:** *What is the opposite of positive 8?* (negative 8) *What is the absolute value of negative 8?* (8)

Assess the Skill

Use the following problems to pre-/post-assess students' understanding of the skill.

integer: _____
opposite: +9
absolute value: _____

integer: –5
opposite: _____
absolute value: _____

integer: 1
opposite: _____
absolute value: _____

STAAR Mathematics Practice Grade 6 • ©2013 Newmark Learning, LLC

Name _____ Date _____

Write an integer to describe each situation. Draw a picture to show each.

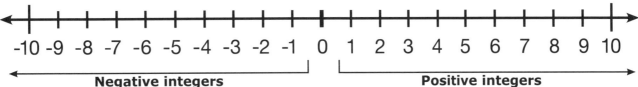

1 4 stories below ground level

_____

2 7 stories above ground level

_____

3 A temperature 20°C above freezing

_____

4 A temperature 5°C below freezing

_____

5 A withdrawal of $75.00

_____

6 A deposit of $150.00

_____

Complete. Use the number line at the top of the page to help you.

7 integer: –4
opposite: _____
absolute value: |4|

8 integer: –3
opposite: _____
absolute value: _____

9 integer: _____
opposite: +2
absolute value: _____

10 integer: –5
opposite: _____
absolute value: _____

11 integer: 1
opposite: _____
absolute value: _____

12 integer: _____
opposite: –16
absolute value: _____

13 integer: 107
opposite: _____
absolute value: _____

14 integer: –90
opposite: _____
absolute value: _____

 Tell how you find the absolute value of –3.

Name _____ Date _____

Write an integer to describe each situation.

1 A deposit of fifty dollars
_____

2 A withdrawal of twenty dollars
_____

3 A decrease in profits of $300
_____

4 Sixteen degrees below zero
_____

5 1,200 meters above sea level
_____

6 A increase in profits of $500
_____

56 meters below sea level
_____

A positive charge of 6
_____

Complete.

7 integer: _____
opposite: +9
absolute value: _____

8 integer: +8
opposite: _____
absolute value: _____

9 integer: –94
opposite: _____
absolute value: _____

10 integer: _____
opposite: –2
absolute value: _____

11 integer: –15
opposite: _____
absolute value: _____

12 integer: +72
opposite: _____
absolute value: _____

13 integer: _____
opposite: +200
absolute value: _____

14 integer: +60
opposite: _____
absolute value: _____

15 integer: +19
opposite: _____
absolute value: _____

 What are negative integers? Explain.

Name _____ **Date** _____

Solve.

1 What integer would represent "ten degrees below zero"?

2 What integer would represent "twenty-two hundred feet above sea level"?

3 What is the opposite of 8?

4 What is the opposite of −45?

5 What is the absolute value of −12?

6 What is the absolute value of −674?

Circle the letter for the correct answer.

7 Which of the following is not an integer?

A 5

B 0

C 0.2

D −2

8 Which integer has an opposite of 9?

A 0.9

B 90

C −9

D 1/9

Unit 4 Mini-Lesson ★
Use Order of Operations

Standard

I. Number, Operations, and Quantitative Reasoning

6.2E (RS) Use order of operations to simplify whole number expressions (without exponents) in problem-solving situations.

Model the Skill

Order of Operations

1. Simplify within parentheses.

2. Multiply and divide from left to right.

3. Add and subtract from left to right.

◆ Write the equation 6 − 4 = 2 on the board. **Say:** *This is an equation. It uses numbers and symbols and an equal sign.* Write the expression 6 − 4 on the board. **Say:** *This is an expression. How is this different from the equation?* (It does not have an equal sign or an answer.) *Today, we will be evaluating expressions. When you evaluate an expression, you find the solution.*

◆ Write the expression 7 x 9 − 4 on the board.

◆ **Ask:** *What do you notice about this expression?* (Possible answer: It has three numbers and two different operation symbols.) *To evaluate this expression, you complete the operations from left to right just as you read words in a sentence. What is 7 multiplied by 9?* (63) *Now you can subtract 4 to finish evaluating the expression. What is 63 minus 4?* (59)

◆ Assign students the appropriate practice page(s) to support their understanding of the skill.

Assess the Skill

Use the following problems to pre-/post-assess students' understanding of the skill.

◆ Ask students to solve each problem.

36 ÷ 9 − 3	50 − 12 x 3	26 − 3 x (14 ÷ 2)
42 x 2 − 1	(8 + 17) x 3	(80 − 3) ÷ 11
63 ÷ (9 − 2)	32 ÷ 8 x 4	5 − 51 ÷ 17

STAAR Mathematics Practice Grade 6 • ©2013 Newmark Learning, LLC

Name _____ **Date** _____

Use the order of operations.
Evaluate each expression.

> **Order of Operations**
> 1. Simplify within parentheses.
> 2. Multiply and divide from left to right.
> 3. Add and subtract from left to right.

1 $5 \times (6 - 3)$

2 $24 \times (4 - 2)$

3 $32 \div (8 - 4)$

4 $28 \div (7 - 3)$

5 $7 \times (7 - 3)$

6 $56 \div (11 - 3)$

7 $3 + (4 \times 3)$

8 $40 + (72 \div 9) \div 8$

9 $23 + (30 \div 10) \times 4$

10 $(24 - 16) \div 8$

11 $32 - 16 \div 8$

12 $4 \times 5 \div 2 - 1$

 Tell how evaluating an expression with parentheses affects the solution.

Name _____ **Date** _____

Use the order of operations. Evaluate each expression.

1 (17 x 2) ÷ (16 ÷ 8)   **2** (25 − 1) + (7 x 2)   **3** (5 x 5) x (6 − 2)   **4** 8 x 8 − 9 x 7

5 (4 x 8) − (9 + 7)   **6** (2 x 8) − 9 + 7   **7** 426 ÷ 3 x 10   **8** 183 − 3 x 50

9 56 + 4 x 6   **10** 178 − (3 x 9)   **11** 5 x (20 − 3) + 8   **12** 49 ÷ 2 + 5

13 4 x 8 + (19 − 3)   **14** 190 ÷ 2 − 2   **15** 76 + 14 x 2   **16** 24 x 4 ÷ 2 x 3

17 56 − (5 x 5 + 5)   **18** 88 − 11 ÷ 11   **19** 12 x 5 + 6 x 3   **20** 135 ÷ 9 − 8 ÷ 2

 Write an explanation of how you evaluated Problem 17.

Name _____ **Date** _____

Solve.

1 Hilary has six times as many apples as James. James has 3 green apples and 4 red apples. How many apples does Hilary have?

2 Kendall has three fewer pencils than Lara. Lara has twice as many pencils as Stephanie. If Stephanie has 10 pencils, how many pencils does Kendall have?

3 There are 13 cars parked in the lot on Wednesday. There are 4 more cars parked on Thursday. There are 5 times that amount on Saturday. How many cars are parked on Saturday?

4 Jaden has 156 baseball cards in a pile. Jaden divides the cards evenly into four albums and then buys 2 more cards to put in each album. How many cards will Jaden have in each album?

5 Brady has 3 dozen eggs. He uses 6 eggs to bake some muffins. Then he uses three times that amount to make omelettes. How many eggs does Brady have left?

6 There are 4 windows in the living room. Each window has 1 set of blinds and 2 panels of curtains. The blinds cost $20 each. Each curtain panel costs $28. How much do the window treatments cost?

Circle the letter for the correct answer.

7 $48 \div 8 - 2 = ?$

    A 2

    B 4

    C 6

    D 8

8 $90 \times 7 - 4 \times 50 \div 2 = ?$

    A 6,750

    B 215

    C 530

    D 3,375

Unit 5 Mini-Lesson ★
Estimate

Standard

I. Number, Operations, and Quantitative Reasoning

6.2D (SS) Estimate and round to approximate reasonable results and to solve problems where exact answers are not required.

6.11A Identify and apply mathematics to everyday experiences, to activities in and outside school, with other disciplines, and with other mathematical topics.

Model the Skill

◆ **Say:** *Estimation is a very useful test-taking strategy. You can estimate a solution to know if the answer is reasonable.* **Ask:** *What are some other ways we use rounded numbers or estimation?* (for example: in science in interplanetary distances; in history and archeology to know the approximate age of artifacts)

◆ **Say:** *Let's estimate the solutions to some travel problems.* Write the following information on the board while you speak. *You're going to drive 1,205 miles from Texas to Wyoming. Your car gets 27 miles per gallon. Gas costs $3.27 a gallon. You are sharing the cost with 3 friends. So far, you have saved $493 for the trip.*

◆ **Ask:** *About how much will gas cost for the trip? What will your share be? If your trip will take about 3 weeks, have you saved enough money for food? About how much money a day (a week, 3 weeks) will you need for food?* Help students estimate by using round or compatible numbers, determining the operation, and estimating the solution.

◆ Assign students the appropriate practice page(s) to support their understanding of the skill.

Assess the Skill

Use the following problems to pre-/post-assess students' understanding of the skill.

Have students estimate.

2,378 + 5,689   11,540 – 7,702   379 x 11   2,168 ÷ 52

Name _____ Date _____

Estimate the solution to each problem.

1

$$25,394 \longrightarrow \boxed{}$$
$$+ \quad 10,705 \longrightarrow + \boxed{}$$

2

$$\$3,210 \longrightarrow \boxed{}$$
$$- \quad 956 \longrightarrow - \boxed{}$$

3

$$415 \longrightarrow \boxed{}$$
$$\times \quad 23 \longrightarrow \times \boxed{}$$

4

$$1,879 \longrightarrow \boxed{}$$
$$\times \quad 11 \longrightarrow \times \boxed{}$$

5 $52)\overline{3,628} \longrightarrow 50)\overline{4,000}$

Or use compatible numbers
$3,500 \div 50 =$ _____

6 $7)\overline{665}$

Compatible numbers
_____ $\div 7 =$ _____

7 $475 + 183 + 500 =$ _____

8 $732 + 151 =$ _____

9 $82 \times 12 =$ _____

10 $3,140 \div 16 =$ _____

11 Mohit spends $12 each week on bus fare. About how much does he spend on bus fare in one year? _____

12 If the Parks drive at an average speed of 58 miles per hour, about how many hours will it take them to drive 469 miles to Flower Mound? _____

13 Is this calculator result reasonable, $736 \times 12 = \boxed{\textbf{1,472}}$?
Explain _____

 Tell how you know if the estimate will be greater or less than the actual amount in Problem 11.

Name _____ Date _____

Estimate the solution to each problem. Tell the method you used.

	Problem	Estimate	Method
1	6,192 + 8,549		
2	$3,095 x 28		
3	$589.99 ÷ 12		
4	$7.83 x 13,098		
5	74,859 – 21,789		
6	25,430,164 + 3,671,277		
7	16,982 – 8,329		
8	37.89 x 6.29		

9 Historic Parker-Cabin in Fort Worth was built in 1848. About how many years ago was it built?

10 Bernard works weekends at the cafe. This weekend he made 83 crepes on Saturday and 129 on Sunday. About how many crepes does he make in a year?

11 This year the Lone Star Chorus concert cost the town $130,732. Concert tickets were $24.95 and the town sold 10,018 tickets. About how much did the town profit from the concert this year in ticket sales?

12 Addy's great grandmother was born in 1917. Addy was born in 2002. About how old was Addy's great grandmother when Addy was born?

13 Each football uniform costs $43. The pads cost $67 and the cleats cost $59. If there are 42 players on the team, about how much do the team's families spend on football equipment? Tell how you know your answer is reasonable.

14 Jesse drove from the Alamo to King Ranch in 3 hours and fifteen minutes. If the driving distance between the two sites is 186 miles, about how fast was Jesse driving?

 Tell how you solved Problem 9.

Name _____ Date _____

Estimate to solve. Use the price list for Problems 1–4.

1 The Wilson family rents a cabin for one week and a canoe for three days. About how much will it cost?

Parks Landing	
Canoe rental	$14/hr
	$35/day
Picnic lunch	$22/person
Cabin rental	$129 per night

2 Eighteen people ordered a picnic lunch. About how much will it cost?

3 Five friends share the cost of renting a cabin for 8 days. If they split it evenly, about how much does each friend pay?

4 Maurice and Dia are staying for 2 days and 3 nights. About how much will it cost for them to rent a cabin, have a picnic lunch each day, and rent a canoe for 3 hours each day?

5 Trevor multiplies 4,278 by 45 and gets a product of 19,251. Is his answer reasonable? Explain why or why not.

6 Timon is making a 2-sided quilt for his grandmother. If he sews about 9 squares a week, and the quilt has 196 squares on each side, about how many weeks will it take him to sew all of the squares?

Circle the letter for the correct answer.

7 Shira exchanged $115 US dollars for Indian rupees. The exchange rate was 57 rupees for each dollar. Which is the best estimate of how many rupees Shira received?

A 5,000 rupees

B 6,000 rupees

C 8,000 rupees

D 10,000 rupees

8 Pilar is driving 148.4 miles to Palo Alto from San Antonio. If she drives at 52 miles per hour the whole way, about how long will it take her to get to her destination?

A 20 minutes

B 3 hours

C 30 hours

D 2 hours

Unit 6 Mini-Lesson ★
Divide Multi-Digit Whole Numbers

I. Number, Operations, and Quantitative Reasoning

6.2C (RS) Use multiplication and division of whole numbers to solve problems including situations involving equivalent ratios and rates.

6.11A Identify and apply mathematics to everyday experiences, to activities in and outside school, with other disciplines, and with other mathematical topics.

Model the Skill

Write the following problem on the board.

$$2,552 \div 4 \qquad 4\overline{)2,552}$$

◆ **Say:** *Today we are going to be dividing multi-digit numbers. Look at the problem. Which number is the divisor?* (4) *Which number is the dividend?* (2,552) *How will you divide 2,552 by 4?* Point out connections to place value and to multiplication by showing how to use the divisor to divide each place–first, the hundreds, then the tens, then the ones.

◆ **Say:** *Now divide 2,552 by 4. Can you tell me the quotient?* (638) Point out how when there aren't enough thousands to divide, you move on to the next place value and try to divide into the hundreds place, and so on.

◆ Assign students the appropriate practice page(s) to support their understanding of the skill.

Assess the Skill

Use the following problems to pre-/post-assess students' understanding of the skill.

2,901 ÷ 12
4,560 ÷ 40
7,291 ÷ 71
8,600 ÷ 24

Name _____ Date _____

Divide. Write the remainder as a whole number or as a fraction in simplest form.

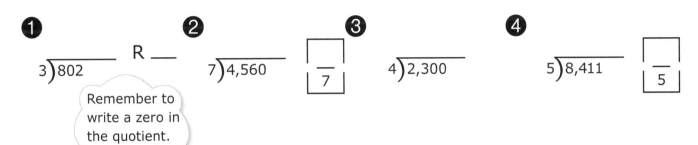

1
_____ R __
3)802

Remember to write a zero in the quotient.

2
_____
7)4,560 $\frac{\boxed{}}{7}$

3
_____
4)2,300

4
_____
5)8,411 $\frac{\boxed{}}{5}$

5
_____
8)2,432

6
_____
10)3,197

7
_____
12)692

8
_____
16)13,604

Divide. Write each remainder as a decimal.

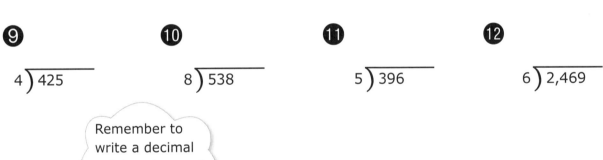

9
_____
4)425

Remember to write a decimal point and zeros to continue dividing.

10
_____
8)538

11
_____
5)396

12
_____
6)2,469

13 512 ÷ 40

14 391 ÷ 17

15 903 ÷ 60

16 444 ÷ 24

 Look at Problem 13. Tell how you can check your answer.

Name _____ **Date** _____

Divide. Write each remainder as a whole number or as a fraction in simplest form.

1 $5\overline{)428}$ **2** $14\overline{)812}$ **3** $20\overline{)1,365}$ **4** $15\overline{)785}$

5 $512 \div 40$ **6** $282 \div 5$ **7** $6,984 \div 4$ **8** $5,428 \div 8$

Divide. Write each remainder as a whole decimal. Round to the nearest hundredth as necessary.

9 $8\overline{)250}$ **10** $16\overline{)1,526}$ **11** $4\overline{)765}$ **12** $48\overline{)954}$

13 $9,430 \div 20$ **14** $3,871 \div 7$ **15** $693 \div 10$ **16** $300 \div 16$

 Show how you divide $20\overline{)3,005}$ **. Label each step.**

 STAAR Mathematics Practice Grade 6 • ©2013 Newmark Learning, LLC

Name _____ **Date** _____

Solve.

1 Sarah earned $114 in 8 hours. How much did she earn per hour?

2 Rafael's grandfather has 126 baseball cards in his collection. If the grandfather gives the same number of cards to Rafael and his two sisters, how many cards does each sibling get?

3 Mike's boat can carry 40 people across the river. Last month 2,504 people rode on Mike's boat. What is the least number of trips that Mike could have made across that river?

4 There are 60 floorboards in the living room. The floor is 14 feet wide. If each floorboard is the exact same width, how wide is each floorboard?

5 Jenna has 300 centimeters of string. She needs 27 centimeters to make a necklace. How many necklaces can she make?

6 The fence is 106 meters long. Each section of fence is 3 meters long. How many sections were needed to complete the fence?

Circle the letter for the correct answer.

7 Anna bought 120 feet of copper wire. She cut it into 16 pieces of the same length. How long is each piece of copper wire?

    A 8 ft

    B 7.8 ft

    C 7.55 ft

    D $7\frac{1}{2}$ ft

8 Oliver buys 258 lbs of rice for his restaurant. He buys 20 bags of rice. How many pounds does each bag hold?

    A 12.6 lbs

    B 12.9 lbs

    C 1.29 lbs

    D 129 lbs

Unit 7 Mini-Lesson ★
Add and Subtract Decimals

Standard

I. Number, Operations, and Quantitative Reasoning

6.2B (RS) Use addition and subtraction to solve problems involving fractions and decimals.

Model the Skill

Draw the following problems on the board.

```
        1.768              1.768
   +    0.834         -    0.834
   _____        _____
```

◆ **Say:** *Today we are going to be adding and subtracting decimals. Look at the first problem. What is the sum?* (2.602) *Explain how you found the sum.*

◆ **Say:** *Now look at the second problem. What is the difference?* (0.934) *Explain how you found the difference.*

◆ **Say:** *Remember to always align the decimal points when you add or subtract. Also remember to always place the decimal point in your answer.*

◆ Assign students the appropriate practice page(s) to support their understanding of the skill.

Assess the Skill

Use the following problems to pre-/post-assess students' understanding of the skill.

```
     3.058          3.058          0.799          0.768
  +  1.431       -  1.431       +  1.04        -  0.08
  _____      _____      _____      _____
```

Name _____ **Date** _____

Use place value. Find each sum or difference.

ones	.	tenths	hundredths	thousandths
	.			
+	.			

Remember to place the decimal point in your answer.

❶
```
    1.07
+   0.89
_____
```

❷
```
    0.3
+   0.75
_____
```

❸
```
    2.265
+   0.834
_____
```

❹
```
    0.508
+   0.09
_____
```

❺
```
    5.25
-   0.79
_____
```

❻
```
    1.2
-   0.7
_____
```

❼
```
    1.8
-   1.671
_____
```

❽
```
    3.891
-   0.054
_____
```

❾ 2.09 + 1.37

_____

❿ 1.15 + 0.95

_____

⓫ 0.08 + 2.26

_____

⓬ 3.61 + 1.49

_____

Remember to align the decimal points when you add or subtract.

⓭ 1.31 - 0.22

_____

⓮ 3.5 - 1.38

_____

⓯ 4.762 - 1.29

_____

⓰ 2.85 + 1.747

_____

 Tell how you use place value to add decimals.

Name _____ Date _____

Find each sum.

1   0.8 + 0.47 = ____

2   0.72 + 0.3 = ____

3   1.5 + 0.8 = ____

4   0.64 + 0.541 = ____

5
```
   1.56
+  1.34
_____
```

6
```
   1.08
+  2.66
_____
```

7
```
   1.405
+  0.79
_____
```

8
```
   0.04
+  1.39
_____
```

9
```
   1.17
+  0.45
_____
```

10
```
   1.4
+  0.67
_____
```

11
```
   1.53
+  0.83
_____
```

12
```
   2.253
+  0.595
_____
```

Find each difference.

13   0.5 − 0.34 = ____

14   0.76 − 0.6 = ____

15   1.4 − 0.07 = ____

16   2.28 − 1.31 = ____

17
```
   6.45
−  0.62
_____
```

18
```
   2.04
−  0.71
_____
```

19
```
   1.95
−  0.99
_____
```

20
```
   0.7
−  0.45
_____
```

21
```
   6.305
−  0.15
_____
```

22
```
   4.28
−  0.98
_____
```

23
```
   0.07
−  0.005
_____
```

24
```
   2.375
−  0.804
_____
```

 Look at Problem 20. How do you know your answer is reasonable?

STAAR Mathematics Practice Grade 6 • ©2013 Newmark Learning, LLC

Name _____ Date _____

Solve.

1 Abby buys a jacket for $37.55 and a skirt for $18.95. What is the total amount she pays?

2 Brittany bought a dozen eggs for $3.98. Alex bought a dozen eggs for $2.49. How much more did Brittany pay for eggs?

3 Luke buys a small pizza for $7.99 and a large pizza with extra cheese for $14.25. How much does he spend on pizza altogether?

4 A small shampoo bottle contains 8.35 ounces. The large bottle of shampoo has 16.5 ounces. How much more shampoo do you get in the large bottle?

5 The concert tickets cost $32.50 each. This price includes a $4.75 service charge for each ticket. What is the face value of the concert ticket without the service charge?

6 The marathon is 26.2 miles long. Jen has run 22.7 miles so far. How many more miles does she have left before she crosses the finish line?

Circle the letter for the correct answer.

7 The temperature rose from 49.3ºF to 65.8ºF. How much did the temperature increase?

    A 115.1ºF

    B 65.8ºF

    C 49.3ºF

    D 16.5ºF

8 Okhee had fifty dollars. She spent $38.63 at the grocery store. Then she spent another $2.89 at the hardware store. How much money does she have left?

    A $35.74

    B $41.52

    C $8.48

    D $11.37

Unit 8 Mini-Lesson ★

Generate Equivalent Forms of Rational Numbers

Standard

I. Numbers, Operations, and Quantitative Reasoning

6.1A (SS) Compare and order non-negative rational numbers.

6.1B (RS) Generate equivalent forms of rational numbers including whole numbers, fractions, and decimals.

Model the Skill

Write the following equivalents on the board.

$$5 = \frac{5}{1} = 5.00 \qquad \frac{1}{4} = 1 \div 4 = 0.25 \qquad 0.75 = 75/100 = \frac{3}{4}$$

◆ **Say:** *We can write equivalent numbers using whole numbers, fractions, or decimals. Look at the first set of numbers.* **Ask:** *How can we write a whole number as a fraction?* (Write 1 as the denominator)

◆ **Ask:** *How can we write a fraction as a decimal?* (Divide numerator by denominator.) Point out that the fraction bar means "divide." **Say:** *Some fractions result in a repeating decimal.* Demonstrate with $1/3 = 0.3333...$ Show students how to write a repeating decimal with a bar over the digit(s) that repeat.

◆ **Ask:** *How can we write a decimal as a fraction?* (Use place value.) Remind students to write the resulting fraction in simplest form, as shown above. Discuss how to use equivalent forms of rational numbers to compare and order decimals and fractions.

◆ Assign students the appropriate practice page(s) to support their understanding of the skill.

Assess the Skill

Use the following problems to pre-/post-assess students' understanding of the skill.

◆ Have students write the decimal or fraction equivalent for each number. Then have them write the numbers from greatest to least.

$$\frac{2}{5} \qquad \frac{3}{8} \qquad \frac{1}{6} \qquad \frac{9}{9} \qquad \frac{9}{1} \qquad 0.2 \qquad 0.6 \qquad 0.50 \qquad 0.35$$

Name _____ **Date** _____

Divide. Write each fraction as an equivalent decimal.

1 $\frac{1}{2}$ $2\overline{)1}$ _____ **2** $\frac{1}{5}$ $5\overline{)1}$ _____ **3** $\frac{1}{8}$ $8\overline{)1}$ _____

4 $\frac{3}{8}$ $8\overline{)3}$ _____ **5** $\frac{7}{10}$ $10\overline{)7}$ _____ **6** $\frac{1}{6}$ $6\overline{)1}$ _____

Use place value. Write each decimal as an equivalent fraction in simplest form.

7 0.9 _____ **8** 0.4 _____ **9** 0.28 _____

10 0.15 _____ **11** 0.75 _____ **12** 1.3 _____

Compare. Use >, <, or =.

13 $\frac{1}{3}$ ◯ 0.55

14 0.35 ◯ $\frac{2}{5}$

15 $\frac{3}{6}$ ◯ 0.5

16 0.7 ◯ $\frac{1}{7}$

17 0.625 ◯ $\frac{5}{8}$

18 $\frac{5}{4}$ ◯ 0.6

 Tell where you would place $\frac{3}{6}$, **0.7, and** $\frac{2}{5}$ **on the number line.**

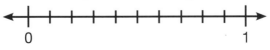

0   1

Name _____ Date _____

Write the fraction or decimal equivalent for each number. Write fractions in simplest form.

1 $\dfrac{3}{8}$ _____

2 $\dfrac{1}{16}$ _____

3 $\dfrac{4}{5}$ _____

4 $\dfrac{2}{3}$ _____

5 $\dfrac{3}{10}$ _____

6 $\dfrac{7}{12}$ _____

7 0.3 _____

8 0.333 _____

9 0.26 _____

10 2.25 _____

11 1.375 _____

12 0.625 _____

Compare. Use >, <, or =.

13 $\dfrac{2}{3}$ ◯ 0.75

14 0.85 ◯ $\dfrac{3}{5}$

15 $\dfrac{3}{4}$ ◯ 0.875

16 0.3 ◯ $\dfrac{1}{5}$

17 0.88 ◯ $\dfrac{7}{9}$

18 $\dfrac{3}{8}$ ◯ 0.4

Write the numbers in order from least to greatest. Place them on the number line.

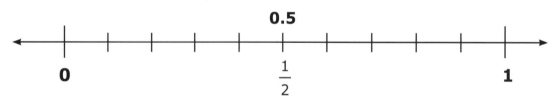

19 $\dfrac{3}{5}$, 0.25, $\dfrac{1}{20}$ _____

20 0.45, $\dfrac{6}{8}$, $\dfrac{12}{12}$ _____

 Tell how you compare decimals and fractions.

Name _____ **Date** _____

Solve.

1 What fraction is equivalent to the decimal 0.4?

2 What fraction is equivalent to the decimal 0.65?

3 What decimal is equivalent to the fraction $\frac{5}{8}$?

4 What decimal is equivalent to the mixed number $3\frac{5}{6}$?

5 What fraction is equivalent to the decimal 1.375?

6 What fraction is equivalent to the decimal 0.416?

Circle the letter for the correct answer.

Breakfast	Number of Orders
Pancakes	37
French Toast	23
Belgian Waffle	40

7 The table shows the breakfast orders of 100 customers at the Pancake House. What decimal represents the fraction of customers that ordered the Belgian Waffle?

A 0.37

B 0.6

C 0.4

D 0.23

8 What fraction represents the portion of customers that did not order pancakes?

A $\frac{2}{5}$

B $\frac{3}{5}$

C $\frac{37}{100}$

D $\frac{63}{100}$

Unit 9 Mini-Lesson ★

Compare and Order Rational Numbers

Standard

I. Number, Operations, and Quantitative Reasoning

6.1A (SS) Compare and order non-negative rational numbers.

Model the Skill

Draw the following number line and problems on the board.

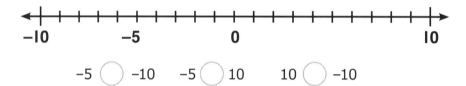

−5 ◯ −10   −5 ◯ 10   10 ◯ −10

◆ **Say:** *Today we are going to be comparing and ordering integers. Look at the number line. Use the number line to tell which number in each expression is greater. Then place the numbers in order. (−10 < −5 < 10)*

◆ **Say:** *Now plot the following points on the number line: −8, 7, −3, 6, 2, −1*

◆ Assign students the appropriate practice page(s) to support their understanding of the skill.

Assess the Skill

Use the following problems to pre-/post-assess students' understanding of the skill.

◆ Ask students to use > or < to make each statement true.

−4 ◯ −18   −12 ◯ 6   3 ◯ −3

◆ Ask students to plot the following points on the number line: -6, 3, 8, -5, -4

Name _____ Date _____

Solve. Then write the integer on the number line.

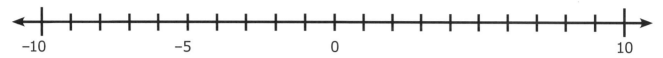

-10   -5   0   10

1 An integer whose opposite is 1 _____

2 An integer whose opposite is 8 _____

> Remember: An opposite integer is an equal distance from 0, but on the opposite side of 0.

3 Two integers whose absolute value is 151 _____

4 Two integers whose absolute value is 27 _____

> Think: Absolute value is a number's distance from 0 on the number line.

Complete the number line above. Write > or < to make each statement true.

5 -9 ◯ -7   6 -2 ◯ -5   7 -6 ◯ -11   8 -4 ◯ -14

> Remember: Numbers to the right on a number line are greater.

9 -12 ◯ -8   10 -7 ◯ -8   11 -13 ◯ -19   12 -16 ◯ -6

13 -5 ◯ -1   14 -3 ◯ -10   15 -6 ◯ 7   16 -4 ◯ -8

17 -23 ◯ -25   18 -73 ◯ -15   19 -18 ◯ -81   20 -2 ◯ 5

 Fractions and decimals are also rational numbers. Tell where you would place $\frac{1}{2}$ and 3.5 on the number line.

Name _____ Date _____

Solve. Then write the integer on the number line.

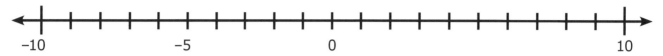

1 An integer whose opposite is 7
_____

2 An integer greater than 7 and less than 9 _____

Solve.

3 An integer whose opposite is 16
_____

4 Two integers whose absolute value is 252 _____

5 An integer whose opposite is −58
_____

6 An integer greater than −10 and less than −8 _____

7 Two integers whose absolute value is 14 _____

8 Two integers whose absolute value is 84 _____

Complete the number line above. Write > or < to make each statement true.

9 −12 ◯ −5

10 −4 ◯ −5

11 −18 ◯ 17

12 −6 ◯ −21

13 −7 ◯ −4

14 −18 ◯ −7

15 −3 ◯ 3

16 −19 ◯ −2

17 23 ◯ −8

18 −13 ◯ −15

19 −41 ◯ −51

20 −17 ◯ −71

21 −10 ◯ −25

22 −23 ◯ −9

23 −6 ◯ 5

24 −3 ◯ −19

 Write how you solved the ninth problem. Draw a picture to prove your answer is correct.

_____

Name _____ **Date** _____

Solve.

1 Which point on the number line is located at −4?

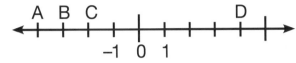

2 Write the integers 4, −7, 5, −2 in order from least to greatest.

3 Which point on the number line is located at 2?

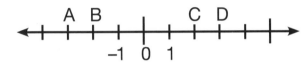

4 Write the integers 12, −14, 10, −20 in order from greatest to least.

5 Which point on the number line is located at −30?

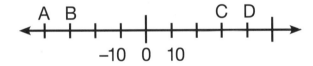

6 Write the integers −143, 125, −118, 60, −36 in order from least to greatest.

Circle the letter for the correct answer.

7 Which statement is true?

    A −15 > −13

    B 12 > −14

    C 10 > 11

    D −11 < −12

8 Which statement is false?

    A −6 < −12

    B −11 < 1

    C 21 < 22

    D −15 < −7

Unit 10 Mini-Lesson ★
Add Fractions

Standard

I. Number, Operations, and Quantitative Reasoning

6.2A (SS) Model addition and subtraction situations involving fractions with objects, pictures, words, and numbers;

6.2B (RS) Use addition and subtraction to solve problems involving fractions and decimals.

Model the Skill

◆ **Say:** *Today we are going to add fractions.* Write $\frac{1}{5} + \frac{2}{5}$ on the board. **Ask:** *How do we add fractions that have the same denominator?* (add the numerators) Have students look at the problem and discuss how they might add the fractions when the denominators are different.

◆ Write $\frac{1}{3} + \frac{1}{6}$ on the board. **Ask:** *What can we do to write these fractions with a common denominator—denominators that are the same? How can we use equivalent fractions?* Help students understand that when one denominator is a multiple of the other denominator, they can simply write an equivalent fraction. Review how to find equivalent fractions by multiplying ($\frac{1}{3} \times \frac{2}{2} = \frac{2}{6}$) or dividing.

◆ Assign students the appropriate practice page(s) to support their understanding of the skill.

Assess the Skill

$$\frac{1}{2} + \frac{1}{2} \qquad \frac{1}{3} + \frac{2}{3} \qquad \frac{1}{4} + \frac{1}{4} \qquad \frac{3}{5} + \frac{1}{5}$$

$$\frac{1}{2} + \frac{2}{3} \qquad \frac{4}{5} + \frac{1}{4} \qquad \frac{5}{6} + \frac{1}{3} \qquad \frac{5}{7} + \frac{2}{5}$$

Name _____ Date _____

Find a common denominator. Add.

1 $\frac{1}{3}$ + $\frac{1}{2}$ $\frac{1}{2}$ × $\frac{3}{3}$ + $\frac{1}{3}$ × $\frac{2}{2}$ = $\frac{3}{6}$ + $\frac{2}{6}$ =   —

2 $\frac{1}{4}$ + $\frac{1}{2}$ $\frac{1}{4}$ + $\frac{1}{2}$ × $\frac{2}{2}$ = $\frac{1}{4}$ + $\frac{2}{4}$ =   —

3 $\frac{3}{4}$ + $\frac{1}{2}$

4 $\frac{5}{6}$ + $\frac{1}{2}$

5 $\frac{3}{6}$ + $\frac{1}{2}$

6 $\frac{1}{6}$ + $\frac{4}{8}$

7 $\frac{7}{8}$ + $\frac{1}{4}$

8 $\frac{3}{8}$ + $\frac{1}{2}$

☆   **Tell how you find the common denominator.**

Name _____ **Date** _____

Find each sum. Use symbols to tell if the sum is greater than (>) or less than (<) 1.

1 $\dfrac{1}{3}$ + $\dfrac{1}{6}$ **2** $\dfrac{3}{4}$ + $\dfrac{1}{2}$ **3** $\dfrac{3}{5}$ + $\dfrac{1}{10}$ **4** $\dfrac{1}{4}$ + $\dfrac{3}{8}$

5 $\dfrac{2}{3}$ + $\dfrac{1}{9}$ **6** $\dfrac{1}{5}$ + $\dfrac{7}{10}$ **7** $\dfrac{1}{8}$ + $\dfrac{1}{2}$ **8** $\dfrac{3}{4}$ + $\dfrac{5}{8}$

9 $\dfrac{5}{7}$ + $\dfrac{1}{5}$ **10** $\dfrac{1}{3}$ + $\dfrac{7}{12}$ **11** $\dfrac{2}{3}$ + $\dfrac{1}{5}$ **12** $\dfrac{1}{6}$ + $\dfrac{6}{9}$

13 $\dfrac{3}{10}$ + $\dfrac{4}{5}$ **14** $\dfrac{1}{8}$ + $\dfrac{5}{12}$ **15** $\dfrac{1}{3}$ + $\dfrac{4}{7}$ **16** $\dfrac{7}{8}$ + $\dfrac{1}{10}$

 Tell how you know if the sum will be greater than 1.

Name _____ Date _____

Solve.

1 What is the sum of $\frac{1}{8}$ and $\frac{3}{4}$?

2 What is the sum of $\frac{2}{5}$ and $\frac{1}{4}$?

3 What is the sum of $\frac{3}{5}$ and $\frac{3}{7}$?

4 The chapter is 8 pages long. Kosta read $\frac{1}{4}$ of the chapter aloud. Then Christina read three pages to the class. How many pages have they read so far?

5 Clara ate $\frac{1}{8}$ of the pie. Jacob ate $\frac{1}{4}$. How much of the pie did they eat in all?

6 The tangerine had 12 sections. I ate five sections. Dad ate $\frac{1}{3}$. How much of the tangerine did we eat?

Circle the letter for the correct answer.

7 The inn has ten rooms. One-half of the rooms are reserved for Friday. The rest are vacant. If 2 more rooms are reserved for Friday, what will be the total number of occupied rooms on Friday?

    A $\frac{5}{12}$

    B $\frac{5}{10}$

    C $\frac{7}{8}$

    D $\frac{7}{10}$

8 What is the sum of seven-eighths and one-sixteenth?

    A $\frac{15}{16}$

    B $\frac{14}{16}$

    C $\frac{7}{8}$

    D $\frac{8}{16}$

Unit 11 Mini-Lesson ★
Subtract Fractions

Standard

I. Number, Operations, and Quantitative Reasoning

6.2A (SS) Model addition and subtraction situations involving fractions with objects, pictures, words, and numbers.

6.2B (RS) Use addition and subtraction to solve problems involving fractions and decimals.

Model the Skill

◆ **Say:** *Today we are going to subtract fractions.* Write $\frac{2}{5} - \frac{1}{5}$ on the board. **Ask:** *How do we subtract fractions that have the same denominator?* (Subtract the numerators.)

◆ **Ask:** *What is the first thing we need to do to subtract fractions with unlike denominators?* (Use equivalent fractions to write common denominators.) Help students find an equivalent fraction for $\frac{1}{3}$ with a denominator of 6. ($\frac{2}{6}$) Review how to find equivalent fractions.

◆ Assign students the appropriate practice page(s) to support their understanding of the skill.

Assess the Skill

Use the following problems to pre-/post-assess students' understanding of the skill.

$$\frac{3}{4} - \frac{1}{2} \qquad \frac{2}{3} - \frac{1}{3} \qquad \frac{3}{4} - \frac{1}{5} \qquad \frac{3}{5} - \frac{1}{5}$$

$$\frac{2}{3} - \frac{1}{3} \qquad \frac{4}{5} - \frac{1}{4} \qquad \frac{5}{6} - \frac{1}{3} \qquad \frac{5}{7} - \frac{2}{5}$$

Name _____ **Date** _____

Find a common denominator. Subtract.

❶ $\frac{1}{2}$ – $\frac{1}{3}$ $\frac{1}{2}$ × $\frac{3}{3}$ – $\frac{1}{3}$ × $\frac{2}{2}$ = $\frac{3}{6}$ – $\frac{2}{6}$ = —

❷ $\frac{3}{4}$ – $\frac{1}{2}$ $\frac{3}{4}$ – $\frac{1}{2}$ × $\frac{2}{2}$ = $\frac{3}{4}$ – $\frac{2}{4}$ = —

❸ $\frac{4}{5}$ – $\frac{1}{2}$

❹ $\frac{5}{6}$ – $\frac{1}{2}$

❺ $\frac{3}{6}$ – $\frac{1}{2}$

❻ $\frac{4}{6}$ – $\frac{4}{8}$

❼ $\frac{7}{8}$ – $\frac{1}{4}$

❽ $\frac{5}{8}$ – $\frac{1}{2}$

 Tell how you found the common denominator.

Name _____ **Date** _____

Solve.

❶ $\dfrac{1}{3} - \dfrac{1}{6}$ **❷** $\dfrac{3}{4} - \dfrac{1}{2}$ **❸** $\dfrac{3}{5} - \dfrac{1}{10}$ **❹** $\dfrac{3}{4} - \dfrac{3}{8}$

❺ $\dfrac{2}{3} - \dfrac{1}{9}$ **❻** $\dfrac{1}{5} - \dfrac{2}{10}$ **❼** $\dfrac{1}{2} - \dfrac{1}{8}$ **❽** $\dfrac{3}{4} - \dfrac{5}{8}$

❾ $\dfrac{5}{7} - \dfrac{1}{5}$ **❿** $\dfrac{2}{3} - \dfrac{5}{12}$ **⓫** $\dfrac{2}{3} - \dfrac{1}{5}$ **⓬** $\dfrac{6}{9} - \dfrac{3}{5}$

⓭ $\dfrac{9}{10} - \dfrac{3}{5}$ **⓮** $\dfrac{7}{8} - \dfrac{5}{12}$ **⓯** $\dfrac{1}{2} - \dfrac{2}{7}$ **⓰** $\dfrac{7}{8} - \dfrac{1}{10}$

 Tell how you could estimate the difference.

Name _____ **Date** _____

Solve.

1 What is the difference between $\frac{3}{5}$ and $\frac{2}{10}$?

2 What is the difference between $\frac{3}{4}$ and $\frac{3}{10}$?

3 What is the difference between $\frac{4}{5}$ and $\frac{3}{8}$?

4 Kim has finished eight of the ten math problems. Phil has finished $\frac{2}{5}$ of the problems. How much more of the math has Kim finished?

5 Cynthia ate $\frac{1}{4}$ of the pizza. If the pizza has eight slices, how many slices are left?

6 The clementine had 12 sections. Noah ate $\frac{3}{4}$ of them. How many sections are left?

Circle the letter for the correct answer.

7 Bella grew $\frac{3}{4}$ of an inch last year. Ben grew $\frac{7}{10}$ of an inch. Who grew more?

    A Bella grew $\frac{1}{20}$ of an inch more.

    B Ben grew $\frac{1}{10}$ of an inch more.

    C Bella grew $\frac{1}{10}$ of an inch more.

    D Ben grew $\frac{1}{20}$ of an inch more.

8 What is the difference between three-twelfths and five-eighths?

    A $\frac{1}{3}$

    B $\frac{3}{8}$

    C $\frac{11}{24}$

    D $\frac{7}{8}$

Unit 12 Mini-Lesson ★
Use Ratios and Equivalent Ratios

Standard

II. Patterns, Relationships, and Algebraic Reasoning

6.3A (SS), 6.2C (RS) Use ratios to describe proportional situations; Use multiplication and division of whole numbers to solve problems including situations involving equivalent ratios and rates.

Model the Skill

Draw the following model on the board.

◆ **Say:** *Today we are going to be finding ratios and equivalent ratios. A ratio shows the relative sizes of two or more values. Ratios can be shown in different ways. A fraction is one way to show a ratio. Look at the circles in this array. Three of the twelve circles are shaded. Write a fraction that shows how many ($\frac{3}{12}$).*

◆ Explain to students that another way to express 3/12 is 3:12 or 3 to 12. Then ask students to think of a way to simplify the expression by writing an equivalent ratio.

$$\frac{3}{12} \quad = \quad 3{:}12 \quad = \quad 3 \text{ to } 12$$

$$\frac{3}{12} \quad = \quad \frac{1}{4} \quad = \quad 1{:}4 \quad = \quad 1 \text{ to } 4$$

◆ Assign students the appropriate practice page(s) to support their understanding of the skill.

Assess the Skill

Use the following problems to pre-/post-assess students' understanding of the skill.

◆ Ask students to use the model below to find the following ratios:

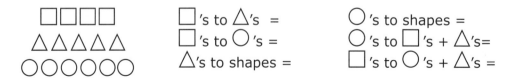

Name _____ Date _____

Write ratios to describe the pictures.

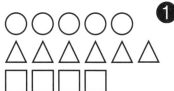

1 circles to shapes

_____

2 triangles to circles

_____

3 circles to squares

_____

4 squares to triangles

_____

5 shaded parts to total parts

_____

6 shaded parts to white parts

_____

Write an equivalent ratio for each. Circle each ratio that is in simplified form.

7 $\dfrac{2}{6}$ = _____

8 $\dfrac{1}{5}$ = _____

9 $\dfrac{12}{24}$ = _____

10 $\dfrac{3}{4}$ = _____

11 $\dfrac{16}{18}$ = _____

12 $\dfrac{4}{6}$ = _____

13 $\dfrac{2}{10}$ = _____

14 $\dfrac{12}{16}$ = _____

15 $\dfrac{5}{8}$ = _____

16 $\dfrac{2}{3}$ = _____

17 $\dfrac{12}{20}$ = _____

18 $\dfrac{25}{30}$ = _____

 Tell how you know that two ratios are equivalent.

Name _____ Date _____

Use the information to write a ratio in simplest form.

1 The class has 14 boys, 12 girls, and 1 teacher.

boys to girls _____ : _____

girls to boys _____ : _____

teachers to students _____ : _____

2 The recipe has 10 tomatoes, 6 cucumbers, and 3 peppers.

tomatoes to peppers _____ : _____

cucumbers to tomatoes _____ : _____

peppers to cucumbers _____ : _____

3 The school has 550 students, 30 teachers, and 10 administrators.

administrators to teachers _____ : _____

teachers to students _____ : _____

administrators to students _____ : _____

4 The math team has 11 boys, 10 girls, and 1 coach.

boys to girls _____ : _____

girls to boys _____ : _____

coaches to students _____ : _____

Use the information to write a ratio in simplest form.

5

●	2	4			10
▲	10		30		

6

●				12	16
▲		6			24

7 $\dfrac{1}{3} = $ _____

8 $\dfrac{2}{10} = $ _____

9 $\dfrac{35}{40} = $ _____

10 $\dfrac{5}{10} = $ _____

11 $\dfrac{12}{18} = $ _____

12 $\dfrac{14}{28} = $ _____

13 $\dfrac{3}{9} = $ _____

14 $\dfrac{2}{3} = $ _____

15 $\dfrac{4}{5} = $ _____

16 $\dfrac{9}{12} = $ _____

17 $\dfrac{75}{100} = $ _____

18 $\dfrac{80}{84} = $ _____

 Explain the steps you take to write the ratio 5:25 in simplest form.

_____

Name _____ **Date** _____

Solve.

1 A fruit salad recipe calls for 9 cups of berries and 6 cups of peaches. What is the ratio of peaches to berries?

2 The pancakes contain 1 cup of milk, 1 cup of flour, and 2 eggs. What is the ratio of milk to flour?

3 There are 25 students in the class. Ten students have sports practice after school. What is the ratio of students that do have practice to those that do not?

4 The baby nursery has 2 nurses for every 10 babies. What is the nurse-to-baby ratio?

5 The island has 600 bicycles and 900 people. What is the bicycle-to-person ratio?

6 The movie multiplex has four bathrooms and 16 theaters. What is the bathroom-to-theater ratio?

Circle the letter for the correct answer.

7 Emi buys 14 balloons. Three are red, four are white, and the rest are blue. What is the ratio of blue balloons to the total number of balloons?

A 11:14

B 2:1

C $\frac{1}{2}$

D $\frac{4}{14}$

8 The cafeteria sold 200 grilled cheese sandwiches, 100 tacos, and 150 grilled chicken salads. What is the ratio of grilled chicken salads sold to the total number of lunches sold?

A 1:2

B 2:1

C 15:300

D 1:3

Unit 13 Mini-Lesson ★

Use Rates

Standard

II. Patterns, Relationships, and Algebraic Reasoning

6.3A (SS), 6.3C (RS), 6.2C (RS) Use ratios to describe proportional situations; Use ratios to make predictions in proportional situations; Use multiplication and division of whole numbers to solve problems including situations involving equivalent ratios and rates.

Model the Skill

Draw the following rates and model on the board.

rate	unit rate
$33/11 lb.	$3/1 lb.
60 mi/2 hr	30 mi/1 hr
6 triangles/3 circles	2 triangles/1 circle

◆ **Say:** *A rate is a ratio that compares two quantities of different increments, or units. For example, 33 dollars for 11 lbs of fruit is a rate. 60 miles per two hours is also a rate. A unit rate reduces the rate so that the denominator is 1. $3 per pound is a unit rate. 30 miles per hour is a unit rate. 6 triangles per 3 circles can be reduced to a unit rate. What is the unit rate in this model?* (2 triangles per 1 circle, or 2/1, or 2:1)

◆ Assign students the appropriate practice page(s) to support their understanding of the skill.

Assess the Skill

Use the following problems to pre-/post-assess students' understanding of the skill.

4 for $32.00

rate: 4 : _____

unit rate: _____ : _____

rate: 30 km/hr

time: 5.5 hours

distance: _____

distance: 360 miles

rate: 15 mph

time: _____

Name _____ Date _____

Complete the ratio tables. Write the unit rate.

1

km		50	150
h	1		6

unit rate ____ : ____

____ km per hour

2 6 for $36.00

unit rate ___ for ___

3 9 : 180

unit rate ____ : ____

4 5 for $46.00

unit rate ___ for ___

5 4 : 240

unit rate ____ : ____

6 35 : 70

unit rate ____ : ____

7 7 : 210

unit rate ____ : ____

8 8 : 64

unit rate ____ : ____

9 10 for $50.00

unit rate ___ for ___

10 3 : 180

unit rate ____ : ____

11 100 for $10.00

unit rate ___ for ___

12 12 : 72

unit rate ____ : ____

Use the formula *D = rt* to find the missing information.

13 rate: 50 miles/hr

time: 2 hours

Distance: _____

14 rate: 30 km/hr

time: 4 hours

Distance: _____

15 rate: 40 km/hr

time: 8 hours

Distance: _____

16 Distance: 400 miles

rate: 40 mph

time: _____

17 Distance: 10 km

rate: 10 kph

time: _____

18 Distance: 30 miles

rate: 15 mph

time: _____

19 Distance: 315 miles

time: 3 hours

rate: _____

20 Distance: 1,400 km

time: 70 hours

rate: _____

21 Distance: 100 m

time: 10 seconds

rate: _____

  Tell the steps you take to find a unit rate.

Name _____ **Date** _____

Find the unit rate.

1 24 : 6

unit rate _____ : _____

2 12 : 96

unit rate _____ : _____

3 80 : 40

unit rate _____ : _____

4 $\dfrac{18}{3}$

unit rate $\dfrac{\Box}{\Box}$

5 $\dfrac{44}{11}$

unit rate $\dfrac{\Box}{\Box}$

6 $\dfrac{42}{6}$

unit rate $\dfrac{\Box}{\Box}$

7 12 for $136

unit rate _____

8 27 ft to 9 yd

unit rate _____

9 6 for $2.40

unit rate _____

Use the formula D = rt.

10 rate: 55 mph

time: 8 hours

Distance: _____

11 rate: 20 mph

time: 6 hours

Distance: _____

12 rate: 30 kph

time: 5 hours

Distance: _____

13 Distance: 90 miles

rate: 15 mph

time: _____

14 Distance: 300 miles

rate: 15 mph

time: _____

15 Distance: 250 km

rate: 50 kph

time: _____

16 Distance: 350 miles

time: 7 hours

rate: _____

17 Distance: 40 km

time: 8 hours

rate: _____

18 Distance: 50 m

time: 25 seconds

rate: _____

19 Distance: 30 miles

time: 30 minutes

rate: _____

20 Distance: 85 km

time: 5 minutes

rate: _____

21 Distance: 200 m

time: 5 minutes

rate: _____

 Explain how you used the formula D = rt to solve Problem 10.

STAAR Mathematics Practice Grade 6 • ©2013 Newmark Learning, LLC

Name _____ **Date** _____

Solve.

1 Look at the sale prices. Which is the better buy? How much does one item cost?

SALE	SALE
5 for $1.00	12 for $3.00

2 Find and compare the unit prices. Which one is the better buy?

SALE	SALE
3 for $1.00	10 for $3.00

---

3 The diner sells bagels for $0.75 each. The bagel shop sells 1 dozen for $7.00. Which is the better buy?

4 The fisherman is selling salmon for $7.99/lb. The supermarket has 2-lb packages of salmon for $14.98. Which is a better buy?

---

5 Cheyenne drove 3,000 miles in 75 hours. At this rate, how long will it take her to drive 4,000 miles?

6 The factory makes 400 cars per day. If the workday is eight hours long, what is the hourly rate at which cars are produced?

Circle the letter for the correct answer.

7 A potter makes 6 bowls in 3 hours. How long would it take the potter to make 14 bowls?

A 6 hours

B 7 hours

C 8 hours

D 9 hours

8 The mechanic does 4 oil changes in 2 hours. How many oil changes can the mechanic do in 8 hours?

A 2 oil changes

B 4 oil changes

C 10 oil changes

D 16 oil changes

Unit 14 Mini-Lesson ★
Understand Percentages

Standard

II. Patterns, Relationships, and Algebraic Reasoning

6.3B (SS) Represent ratios and percents with concrete models, fractions, and decimals.

Model the Skill

Draw the following models on the board.

◆ **Say:** *Today we are going to be finding percentages. A percentage shows the rate per 100. For example, if 40 out of 100 people are wearing white socks, the portion of people wearing white socks would be 40/100, or 40 per 100; therefore 40% of the people are wearing white socks.*

◆ **Say:** *Look at the models. What fraction does each model show? What percent does each model show?*

◆ Assign students the appropriate practice page(s) to support their understanding of the skill.

Assess the Skill

Use the following problems to pre-/post-assess students' understanding of the skill.

◆ Ask students to write percentages that describe each model.

Name _____ **Date** _____

Write a percent to describe each shaded part.

 ❶ 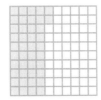   ❷ 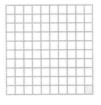   ❸

_____   _____   _____

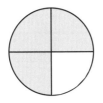 ❹   ❺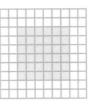

Remember: Percent is a ratio that compares a number to 100. Write an equivalent ratio $\frac{3}{10} = \frac{\square}{100}$

_____   _____

Write each ratio as a decimal and a percent.

❻ $\frac{50}{100}$ ❼ $\frac{65}{100}$ ❽ $\frac{3}{100}$ ❾ $\frac{8}{100}$

_____ _____   _____ _____   _____ _____   _____ _____

❿ $\frac{1}{2}$ ⓫ $\frac{12}{100}$ ⓬ $\frac{5}{100}$ ⓭ $\frac{42}{100}$

_____ _____   _____ _____   _____ _____   _____ _____

⓮ $\frac{1}{100}$ ⓯ $\frac{7}{100}$ ⓰ $\frac{58}{100}$ ⓱ $\frac{23}{100}$

_____ _____   _____ _____   _____ _____   _____ _____

⓲ $\frac{9}{100}$ ⓳ $\frac{15}{100}$ ⓴ $\frac{4}{100}$ ㉑ $\frac{3}{4}$

_____ _____   _____ _____   _____ _____   _____ _____

 ☆   **Tell what 110% means. Draw a picture.**

Name _____ **Date** _____

Write a decimal to describe each shaded part.

① 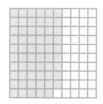   **②** 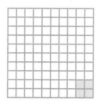   **③**

_____   _____   _____

④ 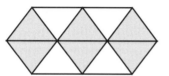   **⑤**   **⑥**

_____   _____   _____

Complete. Write a ratio, decimal, and percent for each.

⑦ ratio $\dfrac{25}{100}$ **⑧** ratio $\dfrac{60}{100}$ **⑨** ratio $\dfrac{3}{10}$ **⑩** ratio $\dfrac{1}{2}$

decimal _____   decimal _____   decimal _____   decimal _____

percent _____   percent _____   percent _____   percent _____

⑪ ratio _____   **⑫** ratio _____   **⑬** ratio _____   **⑭** ratio _____

decimal <u>0.7</u>   decimal <u>0.2</u>   decimal <u>0.08</u>   decimal <u>0.65</u>

percent _____   percent _____   percent _____   percent _____

⑮ ratio _____   **⑯** ratio _____   **⑰** ratio _____   **⑱** ratio _____

decimal _____   decimal _____   decimal _____   decimal _____

percent <u>50%</u>   percent <u>90%</u>   percent <u>2%</u>   percent <u>100%</u>

 Look at Problem 11. In a class of boys and girls, 0.7 represents boys. What percentage represents girls? Explain how you found your answer.

Name _____ Date _____

Solve.

1 Thirty-five girls out of 100 play a musical instrument. What percentage of the girls do not play a musical instrument?

2 Alice got 8 out of 10 questions correct on the quiz. What percentage of the quiz did she get correct?

3 Sean has 125 dollars saved. He pays 25 dollars for a ticket to the concert. What percentage of his savings did he spend on the ticket?

4 On Tuesday, 12 kittens at the shelter were adopted and 4 dogs also found new homes. What percentage of the newly adopted pets at the shelter were dogs?

5 Gabe read 10 books over the summer. 4 were nonfiction. The rest were fiction. What percentage were fiction?

6 Thirty out of fifty questions on the test were multiple choice. What percentage of the questions on the test were not multiple choice?

Circle the letter for the correct answer.

7 Which percent represents the part that is shaded?

   A 0.4%

   B 4%

   C 0.04%

   D 40%

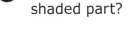

8 Which percent represents the shaded part?

   A $\frac{3}{4}$

   B $\frac{1}{4}$

   C 25%

   D 75%

Unit 15 Mini-Lesson ★
Represent Relationships

II. Patterns, Relationships, and Algebraic Reasoning

6.4A (RS) Use tables and symbols to represent and describe proportional and other relationships such as those involving conversions, arithmetic sequences (with a constant rate of change), perimeter, and area.

6.12A Communicate mathematical ideas using language, efficient tools, appropriate units, and graphical, numerical, physical, or algebraic mathematical models.

Model the Skill

Write the following vocabulary on the board.

variable, expression

◆ **Ask:** *What is a variable?* (a letter or other symbol that represents a number) Discuss student understandings. Create a word map on the board.

◆ **Ask:** *What is an expression?* (a combination of numbers and operation symbols) Show numerical expressions for each operation, then replace one number with a variable to show an algebraic expression, e.g., 2 x 4; $2n$; 6 + (8 – 2); x + (8 – 2) Connect expression to the variable word map.

◆ **Say:** *We can write expressions to represent relationships.* Draw the table below on the board.

input (x)	5	10	15	20
output (y)	4	9	14	19

◆ **Ask:** *What pattern do you see? How can you describe the relationship of output to input?* (output is 1 less than input; subtract 1 from x to get y) Help students write an expression to find y. (x – 1)

◆ Assign students the appropriate practice page(s) to support their understanding of the skill.

Assess the Skill

Use the following problems to pre-/post-assess students' understanding of the skill.

Have students write an expression that could be used to find n.

Number of people	8	16	24	32	p
Number of tables	1	2	3	4	n

($p \div 8$)

Number of boxes (b)	10	12	18	20
Number of crayons (n)	120	144	216	240

($12b$)

Name _____ Date _____

Write an expression to represent each statement.

1 2 times more than s _____

2 2 more than s _____

3 2 less than s _____

4 half of s _____

5 a number n plus six _____

6 a number n divided by ten _____

Write a rule for each table in your own words. Then write an expression that can be used to find y.

7

Input (x)	Output (y)
1	2
3	4
5	6
7	8

rule: _____

expression: _____

8

Input (x)	Output (y)
1	2
3	6
5	10
7	14

rule: _____

expression: _____

9

Club Dues	
Number of students	Number of dollars
4	$60
6	$90
10	$150
15	$225
s	y

rule: _____

expression: _____

10

Height Converter	
Number of inches	Number of feet
144	12
120	10
72	6
48	4
n	y

rule: _____

expression: _____

 Tell how you found the value of n and y in Problem 10.

Name _____ **Date** _____

Complete the table.

	Word Phrase	Variable	Expression
❶	a number increased by 5		$a + 5$
❷	eight times a number	n	
❸			$v \times 7$
❹	a number divided by 2		
❺			$(y + 1) \times 4$
❻	a number decreased by 3		
❼			$(n + 10) \div 6$
❽	a number squared plus 1		

Write a rule for each table in your own words. Then write an expression that can be used to find y.

❾

Input (x)	Output (y)
42	14
27	9
12	4
6	2

rule: _____

expression: _____

Input (x)	Output (y)
1	2
3	10
5	26
7	50

rule: _____

expression: _____

Train Fare

Number of rides	Number of dollars
6	$15
12	$30
24	$60
48	$120
r	y

rule: _____

expression: _____

Measurement Converter

Number of quarts	Number of gallons
72	18
56	14
40	10
24	6
n	y

rule: _____

expression: _____

 What is an algebraic expression? Explain.

STAAR Mathematics Practice Grade 6 • ©2013 Newmark Learning, LLC

Name _____ **Date** _____

Solve.

1 Use the expression $a - 2$ to complete the table.

a	3	5	9	10
b	1			

2 The formula for the perimeter of a rectangle is $P = 2l + 2w$. The perimeter of a rectangular yard is 190 feet. If the width of the yard is 35 feet, what is the length of the yard?

3 The formula for the area of a square is $A = s^2$. The perimeter of a square parking lot is 184 yards. What is the area of the parking lot in square yards?

4 What is the area of the parking lot in square feet?

5 Write an expression that shows how to find the perimeter of the lot in feet.

6 If someone wanted to fence in a lawn that was 17 yards wide and 9 yards long, how many feet of fence would they need to buy?

Circle the letter for the correct answer.

The table below shows how Maya's income changes depending on the number of dogs she walks.

Dog-Walking Income	
Number of dogs	Income (dollars)
5	65
7	91
9	117
10	130
d	n

7 Which expression could be used to find n, the income Maya would earn if she walked d dogs?

A 13d

B $n + 130$

C 65 d

D $n + 26$

Unit 16 Mini-Lesson ★
Generate Formulas

Standard

> **II. Patterns, Relationships, and Algebraic Reasoning**
>
> **6.4B (SS)** Use tables of data to generate formulas representing relationships involving perimeter, area, volume of a rectangular prism, etc.

Model the Skill

Write $P = 4s$ on the board next to a square with each side labeled 5 cm.

◆ **Say:** *A formula is an equation that shows a mathematical relationship. The formula for the perimeter of a square is P = 4s.*

◆ **Ask:** *What does the variable P stand for?* (perimeter) *What does the variable s stand for?* (side) *How can you use the formula to find the perimeter of the square on the board?* (multiply 5 x 4 = 20 cm)

◆ **Ask:** *How does the formula help you find the perimeter of any square?* Help students understand that the formula gives them a rule and that they can substitute the length of one side of any square for *s* to find *P*.

◆ Draw the table below to illustrate the formula. Have students use the table to write a formula for finding the side length, given the perimeter. (*s = P ÷ 4*) Discuss the relationship.

Side length (cm)	3	4	5	6	s
Perimeter	12	16	20	24	P

◆ Assign students the appropriate practice page(s) to support their understanding of the skill.

Assess the Skill

Use the following problems to pre-/post-assess students' understanding of the skill.

Ask students to use the data to write formulas.

x	5	7	11	14
y	8	10	14	17

$y =$ _____ $(x + 3)$

$x =$ _____ $(y - 3)$

Name _____ Date _____

Choose an equation for each problem.

x	5	8	11	15
y	12	15	18	22

y = _____
x = _____

x	41	30	25	22
y	37	26	21	18

y = _____
x = _____

x	10	20	30	40
y	2	4	6	8

y = _____
x = _____

Formulas
$y = x - 4$
$y = \dfrac{x}{5}$
$y = x + 7$
$x = y - 7$
$x = 5y$
$x = y + 4$

Use the data in each table.

4 Write a formula that expresses the relationship between *w*, the weight of water, and *g*, the number of gallons.

w = _____
g = _____

Water

number of gallons	weight (pounds)
2	16
4	32
5	40
10	80
g	*w*

5 Write a formula that expresses the relationship between *s*, the length of a side in a regular hexagon, and *p*, its perimeter.

s = _____
p = _____

Regular Hexagon

length of side (in.)	perimeter
4	24
7	42
9	54
12	72
s	*p*

 For Problem 4, tell how you used the table to write a formula.

Name _____ **Date** _____

Write formulas to represent relationships shown in each table.

1 $y =$ _____

$x =$ _____

x	3	5	7	9
y	18	20	22	24

2 _____

_____

a	9	18	27	36
b	4	13	22	31

3 _____

_____

r	21	35	63	84
s	3	5	9	12

4 This table shows the relationship between the area of a square and the length of one side of the square. Define the relationships.

$A =$ _____
$s =$ _____

Area of a Square

side length (cm)	area (sq cm)
4	16
5	25
6	36
7	49
s	A

5 A rescue group provides food in emergency situations. The table shows how much rice (r) is needed to feed people (p). What formula can the group use to plan how much rice it needs for 1,750 people?

_____

_____

rice (in pounds)	number of people
30	120
50	200
100	400
125	500
r	p

6 A science experiment studying water levels in arid soil yielded these results. Based on the data in the table, what formulas could the scientists use to describe the relationship of this soil (s) and its water content (w)?

_____

_____

soil (in pounds)	water (in mL)
100	5
200	10
300	15
400	20
s	w

 For Problem 4, tell how you used the table to write a formula.

Name _____ **Date** _____

Solve.

1 Using the table, write a formula that expresses the relationship between s, the length of each side of an equilateral triangle, and P, its perimeter.

Equilateral Triangle

Perimeter	Side Length
27	9
45	15
54	18
72	24
P	s

_____

2 What formula can you use, if you know the perimeter of an equilateral triangle, to find the length of its side?

_____

3 This table shows the number of cups of milk (m) to add to pancake mix (p). Write a formula that explains the relationship of cups of milk to cups of mix.

pancake mix (in cups)	milk (In cups)
2	1 1/2
3	2 1/4
4	3
5	3 3/4
p	m

_____

_____

Circle the letter for the correct answer.

4 This table shows the ages of two brothers at different times.

Mike's age *(m)*	13	21	25	42
Dan's age *(d)*	9	17	21	38

Which formula shows the relationship between their ages?

A $m = 4d$

B $m = 2d - 5$

C $d = m + 4$

D $d = m - 4$

5 This table shows the perimeter and area of different squares.

Perimeter *(P)*	16	36	40	44
Area *(A)*	16	81	100	121

Which formula shows how you can use the perimeter to find the area of each square?

A $P = 4s$

B $P = A \div 4$

C $A = (P \div 4)^2$

D $A = (P + s^2)$

Unit 17 Mini-Lesson ★
Write Equations

Standard

II. Patterns, Relationships, and Algebraic Reasoning

6.5A (RS) Formulate equations from problem situations described by linear relationships.

6.12A Communicate mathematical ideas using language, efficient tools, appropriate units, and graphical, numerical, physical, or algebraic mathematical models.

Model the Skill

Write the following equations on the board:

$$y = 4x \qquad a + 3 = d \qquad d/5 = 3 \qquad 27 = d - 12$$

◆ **Say:** *An equation is a mathematical sentence with an equal symbol. It states that the expressions on either side of the equal symbol have the same value. We can write an equation to represent a problem situation.*

◆ **Ask:** *Which equation on the board could represent this situation: I have some donuts. You have 3 more donuts than me. How many donuts do you have?* Guide students' interpretation of the various equations and the selection of $a + 3 = d$.

◆ **Ask:** *What might a problem situation be for $d/5 = 3$?* Discuss that d is divided by 5 and the result is 3. It could represent the number of donuts shared by 5 people. Devise contexts for the other equations on the board.

◆ Write the following problem on the board: Owen ran 24 miles in 5 days. He ran 6 miles each day for the first 3 days. He ran y miles the next day. How many miles did he run the last day, m? Remind students of the order of operations. Guide them to writing the equation $m = 24 - (6 \cdot 3) - y$ (dot for multiplication)

◆ Assign students the appropriate practice page(s) to support their understanding of the skill.

Assess the Skill

Use the following problems to pre-/post-assess students' understanding of the skill.

Ask students to write an equation for each of the following.

• A number, n, is five times more than b.

• A number, y, is 4 more than x.

• Six less than the number of cookies, c, is 31.

Name _____ Date _____

Write an equation to represent each statement.

1 A number, *n*, divided by 3 is 6. _____

2 Two more than a number, *n*, is 16. _____

3 A number, *y*, is two times more than *x*. _____

4 An amount, *a*, is half of *c*. _____

5 A number, *n*, plus 8 is 32. _____

6 A number, *n*, is 4 less than *b*. _____

Choose the equation that represents each problem.

7 Kwame scored 3 more points than Leo. Kwame has 31 points. How many points does Leo have? Let *p* represent the number of points. _____

8 Jen bought 8 pounds of apples for $14.00. What was the price, *p*, per pound?

_____

9 What is *y*?

input	3	6	8	10	*x*
output	5	8	10	12	*y*

_____

10 How much money can Paul earn in *y* hours?

hours	2	4	6	8	*x*
wages	14	28	42	56	*y*

_____

Equations
$p + 3 = 31$
$3p = 31$
$31 - p = 3$
$p + 83 = 14$
$p = 14 - 8$
$8p = 14$
$y = x + 2$
$y = 2x$
$x = 2y$
$x = 56 - y$
$y = 7x$
$yx = 7 + x$

 Tell how an equation is different from an expression.

Name _____ **Date** _____

Write an equation to represent each statement or problem situation.

1 A number, n, divided by 7 is 3. _____

2 A number, y, is 5 more than x. _____

3 A number, s, is half of t. _____

4 8 more than a, multiplied by 2, is equal to b. _____

5 A number, g, multiplied by 2 is 10. _____

6 A number, y, is equal to x squared and then increased by 2. _____

7 Adele is five inches shorter than her sister. Adele is 47 inches tall. How tall is her sister? Use s to represent her sister's height.

_____

8 Will bought 8 pounds of figs for $17.60. Write the formula that shows how to calculate the price (p) per pound. _____
What was the price, p, per pound? _____

9 What is y?

input	3	6	8	14	x
output	7	10	12	18	y

_____

10 This table shows how many hours Toro works (h) to earn different amounts of wages (w). Write the formula that shows how to calculate Toro's hourly wage.

hours	2	4	6	8	h
wages	42	84	126	168	w

_____

 For Problem 7, tell how the equation you wrote describes the situation.

Name _____ **Date** _____

Write an equation for each problem.

1 Erika is thinking of a number. She says her mystery number is 2 more than a number, n, divided by 3. What is Erika's mystery number? Use m to represent Erika's mystery number.

_____

2 The number c is 4 times greater than the number b.

3 Graydon is building a skate ramp. He wants to make sure that he has enough boards. For every foot of height (h), he needs 2 pieces of particle board (b). What formula can he use to calculate his materials (m)?

4 Kristen has 9 days of school before the science fair. She has to convert a number of tables (t) of lab results into graphs for the fair. Write an equation that shows how many graphs (g) she will have to do each day if she wants to finish in time.

5 Yen is training for a marathon. This chart shows his training plan for how many miles he will run each week leading up to the big race. Write a formula that shows the relationship between week (w) and miles run (m).

Week # (w)	Miles (m)
2	8
4	14
6	20
8	26

Circle the letter for the correct answer.

6 Dylan read 210 pages of a book in 5 days. He read 37 pages each day for the first 3 days. He read y pages the fourth day. Which equation can be used to find p, the number of pages Dylan read on the fifth day?

A $p = 210 - 37\,(3 \cdot y)$

B $p = 210 - (37 \cdot 3) - y$

C $p = 210 - 3\,(37 + y)$

D $p = 210 - (y \cdot 3) - 37$

7 Suri is making costumes for the school show. For every costume (c) she needs 2 yards of cloth at $12 per yard, 3 yards of trim at $7 per yard, and 1 yard of ribbon at $5 per yard. Which equation can Suri use to calculate the costume budget (b) for the show.

A $b = c \cdot 36$

B $c = b \cdot (c \times 24 + 21 + 5)$

C $b = c \times 50$

D $c = b \times 48$

Unit 18 Mini-Lesson ★
Classify Triangles

Standard

III. Geometry and Spatial Reasoning

6.6A (SS) Use angle measurements to classify angles as acute, obtuse, or right.

6.6B (SS) Identify relationships involving angles in triangles and quadrilaterals.

6.13A Make conjectures from patterns or sets of examples and nonexamples.

Model the Skill

Draw and label the following triangles on the board.

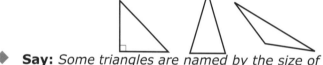

◆ **Say:** *Some triangles are named by the size of their angles. A right triangle has 1 right angle.* Point to the right angle. *A right angle measures 90 degrees. The rays that form the right angle are perpendicular.*

◆ **Ask:** *What can you tell me about the angles in the acute triangle?* (3 angles, no right angles) *Are the sizes of the angles greater or less than 90º?* (less) Have students use the corner of a page to compare a right angle with the angles in the acute triangle. Point out that all 3 angles are acute in an acute triangle.

◆ **Ask:** *What can you tell me about the angles in the obtuse triangle?* (3 angles, no right angles) *Are the sizes of the angles greater or less than 90º?* (1 angle is greater and 2 are less) Allow students to compare the angles to a right angle. Note that an obtuse triangle has 1 obtuse angle.

◆ **Say:** *In any triangle the sum of the angle measures is 180 degrees.* Write 90º and 45º on the right triangle. *If we know the measure of two angles, we can find the measure of the third angle.* Help students find the missing angle measure and determine if the angle is acute or obtuse.

◆ Assign students the appropriate practice page(s) to support their understanding of the skill.

Assess the Skill

Use the following problems to pre-/post-assess students' understanding of the skill.

Have students classify each triangle as right, obtuse, or acute.

Name _____ Date _____

Classify each triangle as acute, obtuse, or right.

❶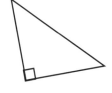

_____

❷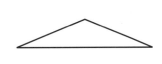

_____

❸

_____

❹

_____

❺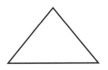

_____

❻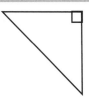

_____

❼

_____

❽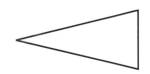

_____

❾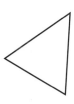

_____

Solve.

❿ If two angles of a triangle are each 45°, what kind of triangle is it? _____

⓫ What is the measure of angle ∠ A? _____

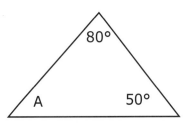

 Tell how you know if a triangle is an acute triangle.

Name _____ **Date** _____

Classify each triangle as acute, obtuse, or right.

 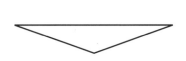

_____

_____

_____

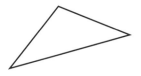

_____

_____

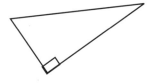

_____

Solve.

7 All triangles have 3 angles. What is the sum of their measures?

_____

8 What is the measure of all three angles in an equilateral triangle?

9 What is the measure of angle ∠ B?

_____

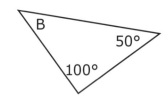

10 What is the measure of angle ∠ G?

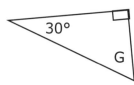

11 In a right triangle, the right angle is always equal to the sum of the other angles. True or false?

_____.

12 In an obtuse triangle, the hypotenuse is always opposite the triangle's _____ angle.

 Tell how you found the missing measure of an angle in Problem 10.

Name _____ Date _____

Solve.

1 Which triangle is an acute triangle? Tell how you know.

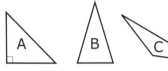

_____
_____

2 Which triangle has no obtuse angles? Tell how you know.

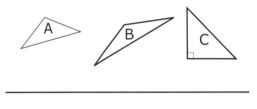

_____
_____

3 If two angles of a triangle are each 35°, what is the measure of the third angle?

4 If one angle of a right triangle is 65°, what is the measure of the third angle?

5 What is the measure of angle C?

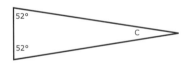

6 If angle N is 40°, what is the measure of angle M?

Circle the letter for the correct answer.

7 Which statement about triangles is NOT true?

A If all the angles of a triangle are congruent, then the measure of each angle is 60°

B If a triangle has a right angle, then both of the other angles are acute.

C If a triangle has an obtuse angle, then both of the other angles are acute.

D If a triangle has an acute angle, then one of the other angles must be right or obtuse.

8 If angle Q is ten degrees less than angle R, what is the measure of angle S?

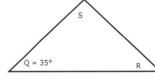

A 100°

B 90°

C 80°

D 55°

Unit 19 Mini-Lesson ★
Quadrilaterals

Standard

III. Geometry and Spatial Reasoning

6.6B (SS) Identify relationships involving angles in triangles and
quadrilaterals.

6.13A Make conjectures from patterns or sets of examples and
nonexamples.

Model the Skill

Draw and label the following quadrilaterals on the board.

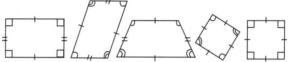

◆ **Say:** *We learned about polygons with 3 sides and 3 angles—triangles.* ("tri"
meaning 3) *Today we are going to learn about polygons with 4 sides and 4
angles—quadrilaterals.* ("quad" meaning 4) *Look at the quadrilaterals on the
board.*

◆ **Ask:** *What can you tell me about the first one?* (rectangle; opposite sides
congruent and parallel; 4 right angles) Write properties under the shape as
they are discussed. Continue in the same fashion for all the quadrilaterals:

  • Parallelogram (opposite sides congruent and parallel; opposite angles are
    congruent) Ask: *Is a rectangle a parallelogram?* (yes)

  • Trapezoid (exactly one pair of parallel sides)

  • Rhombus (a parallelogram; opposite angles congruent; 4 congruent sides)

  • Square (a rectangle; 4 right angles with 4 congruent sides)

◆ **Ask:** *What do you think the sum of the angle measures of a rectangle is?*
(360º)

◆ *Is that true for all quadrilaterals?* (yes) Guide students to see that every
quadrilateral can be divided into exactly two triangles by drawing a diagonal.
Remind students that the sum of the measures of the angles in a triangle is
180º (180 x 2 = 360)

◆ Assign students the appropriate practice page(s) to support their
understanding of the skill.

Assess the Skill

Use the following problems to pre-/post-assess students'
understanding of the skill.

Have students identify angle relationships for each figure and name the
quadrilateral.

STAAR Mathematics Practice Grade 6 • ©2013 Newmark Learning, LLC

Name _____ Date _____

Match each quadrilateral to its properties.

①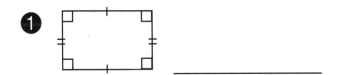

_____

②

_____

③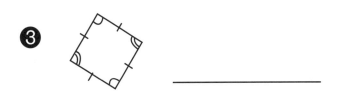

_____

④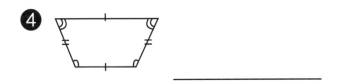

_____

A. Opposite angles are congruent and parallel.

B. Has exactly one pair of parallel sides.

C. Has 4 right angles and opposite sides are congruent and parallel.

D. Has 4 right angles and 4 congruent sides.

E. Opposite angles are congruent and opposite sides are parallel; all sides are congruent.

Find the missing angle measure.

⑤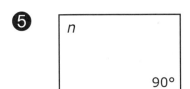

The measure of ∠ n is _____

⑥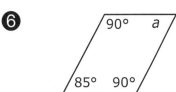

The measure of ∠ a is _____

⑦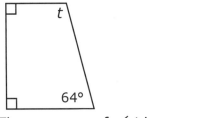

The measure of ∠ t is _____

⑧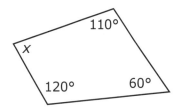

The measure of ∠ x is _____

 Tell how you know if a triangle is an acute triangle.

Name _____ Date _____

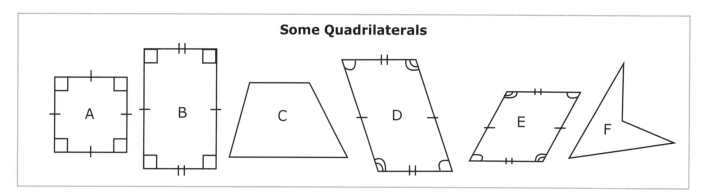

Some Quadrilaterals

Write the name that best describes each quadrilateral.

❶ A: _____

❷ B: _____

❸ C: _____

❹ D: _____

❺ E: _____

❻ F: _____

List all of the quadrilaterals above that have the following properties:

❼ 4 congruent sides

_____

❽ 2 pairs of parallel sides

_____

❾ congruent opposite angles

_____

❿ 4 right angles

_____

Find the missing angle measure.

⓫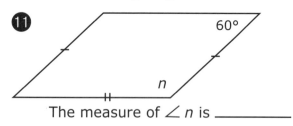

The measure of ∠ n is _____

⓬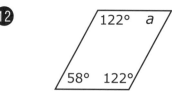

The measure of ∠ a is _____

⓭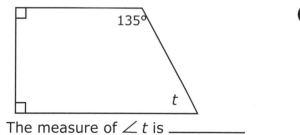

The measure of ∠ t is _____

⓮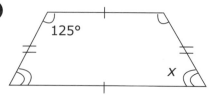

The measure of ∠ x is _____

 Tell which quadrilaterals can be classified as parallelograms.

Name _____ **Date** _____

Solve.

1 Which quadrilaterals must have perpendicular sides? Explain.

2 Which quadrilaterals must have at least one set of parallel sides? Explain.

3 Which quadrilaterals have two sets of congruent sides?

4 Which quadrilaterals have 4 congruent sides?

5 What is the measure of angle J?

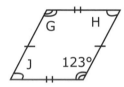

6 What is the measure of angle C?

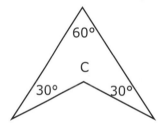

Circle the letter for the correct answer.

7 Which statement about quadrilaterals is NOT true?

A If the angles in a quadrilateral are congruent, then the measure of each angle is 90°.

B If a quadrilateral has exactly 2 obtuse angles, then each of the other angles is a right angle.

C If a figure is a parallelogram, then its opposite angles are congruent.

D If a figure is a rhombus, then its parallel sides are congruent.

8 Which polygon is a trapezoid?

A

B

C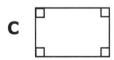

D

Unit 20 Mini-Lesson ★

Circles

Standard

III. Geometry and Spatial Reasoning

6.6C (RS) Describe the relationship between radius, diameter, and circumference of a circle.

Model the Skill

Draw the following circles on the board:

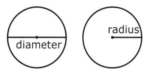

◆ **Ask:** *How would you describe the diameter of a circle?* (a segment connecting 2 endpoints on the circle and passing through the center) Draw a chord on the circle. **Ask:** *Is this segment a diameter?* (no) Tell students that a diameter must pass through the center. Label the line segment AB

$$\overline{AB}$$

◆ **Ask:** *How would you describe the radius of a circle?* (a segment with one endpoint on the circle and another at the center) *What is the relationship of the radius to the diameter?* (it is 1/2 the diameter)

◆ **Say:** *The distance around a circle is called the* **circumference.** *The length of the diameter determines the circumference.* Draw a circle with a diameter of 5 inches. Use a piece of string to measure the circumference of the circle. Mark the string and lay it flat. Guide students to see how many times a 5-inch segment can be laid end-to-end along the circumference. (about 3 times) If there is time, give students string and a ruler and allow them to explore relationships of diameter, radius, and circumference of various circles.

◆ Assign students the appropriate practice page(s) to support their understanding of the skill.

Assess the Skill

Use the following problems to pre-/post-assess students' understanding of the skill.

Ask students to use the circle below to define each segment.

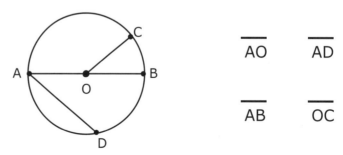

STAAR Mathematics Practice Grade 6 • ©2013 Newmark Learning, LLC

Name _____ **Date** _____

Use the circle to answer each question.

1 Which line segment is the diameter of the circle?

_____

2 What is the center point of the circle?

_____

3 What part of the circle is line segment $\overline{EO}$?

_____

4 How many line segments can you find that form a radius? List them.

_____

5 What part of the circle is line segment $\overline{FG}$?

_____

6 If the diameter of a circle is 20 meters, how many meters long is the radius?

_____

7 If the radius of a circle is 4.5 meters, how many meters long is the diameter of the circle?

_____

8 If the line segment $\overline{OE}$ of the circle at the top of the page is 3 inches long, how long is the diameter?

_____

9 Brent says that if $\overline{OE}$ is 3 inches long, then the circumference of the circle is about 18 inches. Is he correct? Explain.

_____

☆ **Tell what circumference means.**

_____

_____

Name _____ **Date** _____

Write the name for each part of the circle.

1 line segment $\overline{AC}$ **2** Point E   **3** $\overline{AB}$

_____   _____   _____

4 $\overline{DE}$ **5** $\overline{DA}$ **6** $\overline{EB}$

_____   _____   _____

Write true or false.

7 Every radius in a circle is congruent. _____

8 The diameters of two congruent circles are equal. _____

9 The chord is always the radius. _____

Solve.

10 If the diameter of a circle is 650 centimeters, how many centimeters long is the radius?

_____

11 If the line segment $\overline{EC}$ of the circle at the top of the page is 5 1/2 inches long, how long is the diameter?

_____

12 Use the table to write a formula that represents the relationship of circumference, c, to diameter, d

c = _____

Circle Measurements

Diameter	Circumference
2	6.28
3	9.42
4	12.56
5	15.7
10	31.4
d	c

 Tell what the relationship is between the circumference and diameter of a circle.

   STAAR Mathematics Practice Grade 6 • ©2013 Newmark Learning, LLC

Name _____ **Date** _____

Solve.

1 The radius of a circle is 4 meters. What is the diameter?

2 The diameter of a circle is 12 inches. What is the radius?

3 The diameter of a circle is 41 meters. What is the radius?

4 The radius of a circle is 3.75 meters. What is the circumference?

Circle the letter for the correct answer.

5 The diameter of a circle is 74 centimeters.

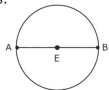

What is the measure of the radius?

    A 24.7 cm

    B 37 cm

    C 148 cm

    D 222 cm

6 The radius $\overline{OC}$ is 10 inches.

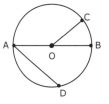

What is the circumference of the circle?

    A 3.14 in

    B 31.4 in

    C 62.8 in

    D 6.28 in

Unit 21 Mini-Lesson ★

Locate Points on the Coordinate Plane

Standard

III. Geometry and Spatial Reasoning

6.7A (SS) Locate and name points on a coordinate plane using ordered pairs of non-negative rational numbers.

Model the Skill

Draw the coordinate plane on the board and list the following coordinates in written and table form.

A (3, 5)   B (5, 6)   C (7, 7)   D (9, 8)

x	y
3	5
5	6
7	7
9	8

◆ **Say:** *We can use ordered pairs, or coordinates, to plot points. The first number in the ordered pair (x) tells how far to move along the x-axis. The second number (y) tells how far to move along the y-axis.* Point A is at (3, 5). Have students plot points A–D and connect the points to form a line.

◆ Assign students the appropriate practice page(s) to support their understanding of the skill.

Assess the Skill

Use the following problems to pre-/post-assess students' understanding of the skill.

◆ Have students graph the following coordinates on the coordinate plane.

A (3, 5)
B (5, 3)
C (8, 5)
D (6, 7)

x	y
1	2
2	4
3	6
4	8

x	y
3	2
5	4
7	6
9	8

STAAR Mathematics Practice Grade 6 • ©2013 Newmark Learning, LLC

Name _____ Date _____

Graph and label the following points using the (*x, y*) coordinates.

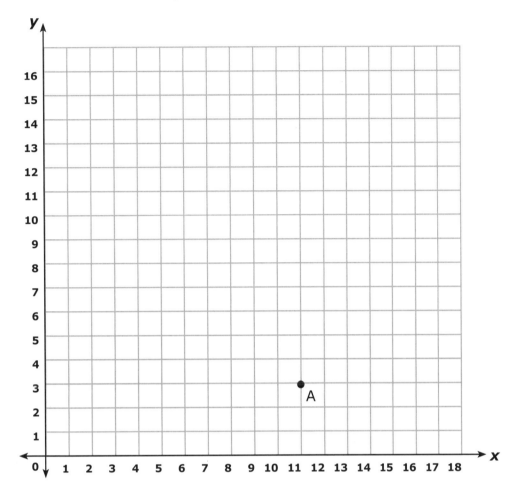

1 Point A: (11, 3)

2 Point B: (11, 5)

3 Point C: (8, 5)

4 Point D: (8, 3)

5 Point E: (2, 12)

6 Point F: (12, 2)

7

hours (*x*)	3	4	5	6
dollars (*y*)	5	6	7	8

8

x	*y*
6	12
8	10
10	8
12	6

☆ **Tell how you use an ordered pair to graph a point.**

Name _____ Date _____

Graph each point.

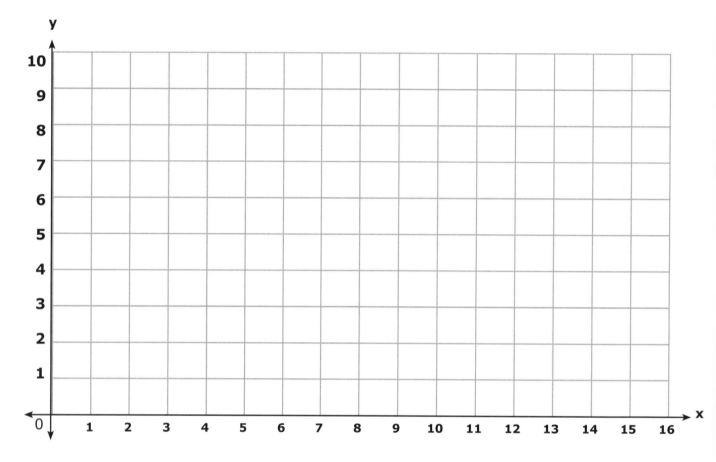

❶ Point J: (1, 7)

❷ Point K: (2, 9)

❸ Point L: (4, 9)

❹ Point M: (5, 7)

❺ Point N: (4, 5)

❻ Point O: (2, 5)

❼ Connect points JKLM and describe the shape.

❽

quarts (x)	4	8	12	16
gallons (y)	1	2	3	4

❾

pints (x)	2	4	6	8
quarts (y)	1	2	3	4

❿

x	y
11	9
11	8
11	7
11	6

 Explain why K is a point, KL is a line segment, and y = 9 is a line.

Name _____ **Date** _____

Solve.

1 Use the ordered pair in the table to graph point A on the coordinate plane.

x	y
1	7

2 Graph triangle DEF using the following coordinates: (4, 2), (8, 2), and (8, 4)

3 Graph the line $x = y + 1$ using the coordinates in the table.

x	2	3	4	5
y	1	2	3	4

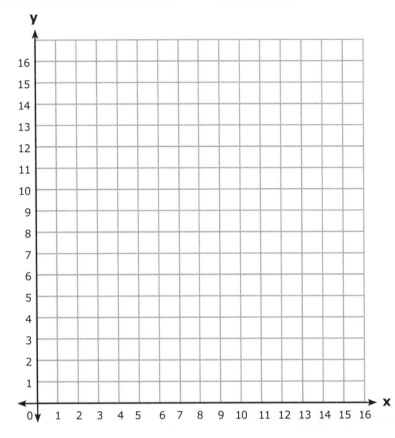

4 In 1 hour, factory workers can make 4 cars. In 2 hours, they can make 8 cars. In 4 hours, they can make 16 cars. Complete the table. Then graph the points in the table.

input	output
x	y
1	4
2	
3	
4	

Circle the letter for the correct answer.

5 How many cars can the factory workers make in 10 hours?

A 10

B 40

C 48

D 56

6 Which of the following points is on the line $y = 4x$?

A (8, 2)

B (4, 12)

C (5, 20)

D (20, 5)

Unit 22 Mini-Lesson
Measure Angles

Standard

IV. Measurement

6.8C (SS) Measure angles.

Model the Skill

Draw a right angle on the board.

◆ **Say:** *We are going to find some right angles in our classroom. A right angle looks like the corner of this page.* Remind students that an angle is formed by two rays with the same vertex and that perpendicular lines form right angles.

◆ **Ask:** *What right angles can you see in our room?* (corners of windows, doors, books, etc.) Draw a circle on the board with perpendicular lines through the center to create four right angles. Relate angle measures to turns. **Say:** *We measure angles in degrees. A right angle measures 90 degrees. A right angle is a quarter turn.*

◆ Demonstrate how to use the corner to determine which angle is greater than, less than, or equal to 90º. Point out that angles are named by their relationship to a right angle.

◆ Assign students the appropriate practice page(s) to support their understanding of the skill.

Assess the Skill

Use the following problems to pre-/post-assess students' understanding of the skill.

◆ Ask students to draw examples of right, acute, and obtuse angles.

◆ Then have them use a protractor to measure and describe the following angles.

Name _____ Date _____

Use a protractor. Measure each angle.

1 Angle ∠ CBD measures

_____ degrees.

2 Angle ∠ ABC measures

_____ degrees.

3 Angle ∠ ABD measures

_____ degrees.

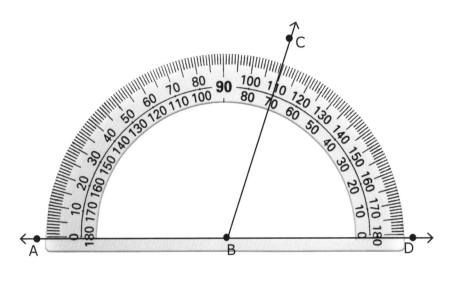

4 ∠ EFG measures _____.

5 ∠ HIJ measures _____.

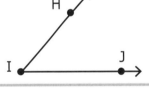

6 ∠ KLM measures _____.

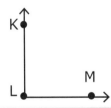

7 ∠ NOP measures _____.

8 ∠ XYZ measures _____.

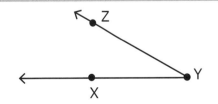

 Tell how you use a protractor.

Name _____ **Date** _____

Use a straight edge. Draw an angle for each problem. Use the diagram to help.

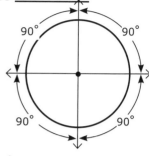

❶ Sketch an angle that measures about 90º.

❷ Sketch an angle that measures less than 90º.

❸ Sketch an angle that measures about 45º.

❹ Sketch an angle that measures about 140º.

❺ Sketch an angle that measures about 180º.

❻ Sketch an angle that measures about 225º.

 In Problem 6, tell how you know the angle is about 225º.

Name _____ **Date** _____

Solve.

1 Which angle is greater than 90º?

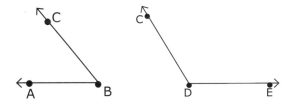

2 Sketch a right angle.

3 If you divide this half-circle into six equal angles, what will be the measure of each angle?

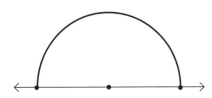

4 Use a protractor to measure. What is the measure of angle QXR?

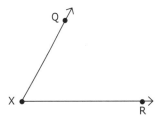

Circle the letter for the correct answer.

5 The ∠ XYZ measures 100º. What is the measure of ∠ WYZ?

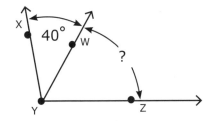

A 40º

B 60º

C 80º

D 140º

6 What is the measure of ∠ KMN?

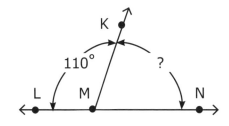

A 250º

B 140º

C 90º

D 70º

Unit 23 Mini-Lesson ★
Convert Measures

Standard

IV. Measurement

6.8D (SS) Convert measures within the same measurement system (customary and metric) based on relationships between units.

6.11B Use a problem-solving model that incorporates understanding the problem, making a plan, carrying out the plan, and evaluating the solution for reasonableness.

Model the Skill

◆ Post or write on the board both metric and customary equivalent units for length, weight/mass, and capacity. Have students copy them into a notebook for reference and use.

◆ **Ask:** *If I have a board 100 centimeters long, how many meters long is it?* (1 meter) *What if the board is 3 feet long? How many yards long is it?* (1 yard) *How do you know the answer to these questions?* (we can convert among units within the same system)

◆ **Say:** *In the metric system, which is used in most of the world, the conversions are based on the decimal system, so, for example, 1,000 grams is equivalent to 1 kilogram, and 500 grams is equal to 0.5 kilogram.* Using metric equivalents, have students make up and solve conversion problems.

◆ **Say:** *Converting customary measures is not so easy. We need to remember how many cups are in a quart* (4) *and how many ounces are in a pound.* (16) **Ask:** *How would you solve this problem?*

We need 8 1/2 feet of tape to mark a starting line for a race. We have 1 1/3 yards of tape on one roll and 45 inches of tape on another roll. If we need more tape, how much more do we need? (9 in. or 3/4 ft]

◆ Guide students to develop a plan, determine how to find a common unit, and decide how to express the answer. If students are not sure of the relationships between units, allow them to use their reference chart.

◆ Assign students the appropriate practice page(s) to support their understanding of the skill.

Assess the Skill

Use the following problems to pre-/post-assess students' understanding of the skill.

365 cm = _____ m   2.5 L = _____ mL   3,000 g = _____ kg

78 in. = _____ ft   5 gal = _____ qt   3 lbs. = _____ oz

STAAR Mathematics Practice Grade 6 • ©2013 Newmark Learning, LLC

Name _____ Date _____

Convert metric units.

1 5 m = _____ cm
5 x _____ = _____

2 800 cm = _____ m
800 ÷ _____ = _____

3 350 cm = _____ m
350 ÷ _____ = _____

4 6 km = _____ m
6 x _____ = _____

5 1,750 g = _____ kg
1,750 ÷ _____ = _____

6 4.3 kg = _____ g
4.3 x _____ = _____

7 2.25 L = _____ mL
2.25 x _____ = _____

8 5,000 mL = _____ L
5,000 ÷ _____ = _____

Metric Units
Length
1 centimeter (cm) = 10 mm
1 meter (m) = 100 cm
1 kilometer (km) = 1,000 m
Mass
1 gram (g) = 1,000 mg
1 kilogram (kg) = 1,000 g
Capacity
1 liter (L) = 1,000 mL

Convert customary units.

9 15 ft = _____ yd
15 ÷ _____ = _____

10 5 ft = _____ in.
5 x _____ = _____

11 2 mi = _____ yd
2 x _____ = _____

12 64 oz = _____ lbs.
64 ÷ _____ = _____

13 3 t = _____ lbs.
3 x _____ = _____

14 5 pt = _____ c
5 x _____ = _____

15 10 qt = _____ gal
10 ÷ _____ = _____

16 3 qt = _____ c
3 x _____ = _____

Customary Units
Length
1 foot (ft) = 12 inches (in.)
1 yard (yd) = 3 ft
1 mile (mi) = 1,760 yd
Weight
1 pound (lb) = 16 ounces (oz)
1 ton (t) = 2,000 lbs.
Capacity
1 cup (c) = 8 fluid ounces
1 pint (pt) = 2 c
1 quart (qt) = 2 pt
1 gallon (gal) = 4 qt

 Tell the operation you use to convert from a larger unit to a smaller unit.

Name _____   **Date** _____

Complete.

1 60 m = _____ cm   **2** 72 km = _____ m   **3** 4.5 cm = _____ mm

4 250 g = _____ mg   **5** 5.8 km = _____ m   **6** 750 mL = _____ L

7 87 L = _____ mL   **8** 4,008 m = _____ cm   **9** 18,900 m = _____ km

10 98 c = _____ gal   **11** 7 mi = _____ yd   **12** 8,400 lbs. = _____ t

13 48 lbs. = _____ oz   **14** 195 ft = _____ yd   **15** 15 yd = _____ in

16 753 ft = _____ yd   **17** 84 qt = _____ gal   **18** 16 gal = _____ pt

19 Elena buys 3,500 grams of grapes. How many kilograms is that?

20 Andy runs 5 miles. How many yards is that?

  Tell the operation you use to convert from a smaller unit to a larger unit.

Name _____ **Date** _____

Solve.

1 Robyn bought 32 ounces of orange juice. How many quarts of juice is that?

2 If Hector ran 35.5 kilometers last week and 22.5 kilometers this week, how many meters did he run over the last two weeks?

3 The boat weighs 6,628 pounds. The tow hitch can safely pull a maximum of 3 tons. Can the tow hitch safely tow the boat?

4 The salt factory has 2 tons of table salt ready to be packaged. If the salt is packaged in 16-ounce containers, how many containers can be filled?

5 The dresser is 78 inches long. The length of the bedroom wall between the two closets is 7 feet. If the dresser is centered on the wall between the two closets, how many inches will separate the dresser and the closet on either side?

6 For her science project, Flora has to dilute 100 mL of solvent into every 2 liters of water. How many liters of solvent would she need to dilute into 10 liters of water?

Circle the letter for the correct answer.

7 Jake is making broth for his famous Thanksgiving soup. The recipe calls for 1 bouillon cube for every quart of soup. If he ends up making 16 pints of soup, how many cubes will he have used?

    A 4 cubes

    B 16 cubes

    C 8 cubes

    D 32 cubes

8 The town half-marathon is 13.1 miles long. If the town has to place 2 cones every 2 yards along the course, how many cones will the town need to complete the course?

    A 13,100 cones

    B 23,056 cones

    C 11,528 cones

    D 5,764 cones

Unit 24 Mini-Lesson ★

Solve Problems Involving Measurements

Standard

> **IV. Measurement**
>
> **6.8B (RS)** Select and use appropriate units, tools, or formulas to measure and to solve problems involving length (including perimeter), area, time, temperature, volume, and weight.

Model the Skill

Display measuring tools such as rulers, scales, clocks, and thermometers. Review how to use them.

◆ **Say:** *Today, we are going to solve problems involving length, weight, time, and temperature. Some problems may require measurement with an appropriate tool. Others may require converting units of measure.*

◆ Write this problem on the board: *I have two sections of fence. One section is $3\frac{1}{2}$ ft long. The other is 57 inches long. I need to fence one side of my garden that is 10 feet long.*

◆ **Ask:** *What is the total length of the fence sections?* (99 in. or $8\frac{1}{4}$ ft) *How much more fencing will I need?* ($1\frac{3}{4}$ ft or 21 in.) Discuss how to add and subtract measurements. Note that they must be like measures and students will need to convert units.

◆ **Say:** *It is 10:03 AM now and the temperature is 68 degrees Fahrenheit.* (Use actual time and temperature) **Ask:** *What time will it be in 3 hours and 25 minutes?* (1:28 PM) *If the temperature rises 17 degrees in that time, how hot will it be?* (85°F)

◆ Have students use measuring tools to create and solve other similar problems.

◆ Assign students the appropriate practice page(s) to support their understanding of the skill.

Assess the Skill

Use the following problems to pre-/post-assess students' understanding of the skill.

358 cm + 2.5 m = _____ m   5 h 45 min – 1 1/2 h = _____ h _____ min

650 g x 4 = _____ kg   32°C – 17°C = _____ °C

Name _____ **Date** _____

Solve.

1   2.5 h – 1 h 48 min = _____ min

2   412 g x 10 = _____ kg

3   5 lb ÷ 4 = _____ oz

4   3 lb 7 oz + 12 oz = ____ lb ____ oz

5   6 ft ÷ 8 = _____ in

6   23°C – 15°C = _____ °C

---

7   Mr. Foster is a teacher. He drives past the library going to and from school. How many km does he drive round trip?

_____

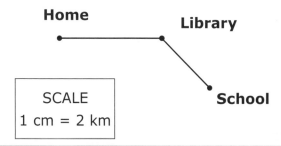

SCALE
1 cm = 2 km

---

8   The kitchen clock loses 1 minute every 12 hours. How many days will it take for the clock to be 10 minutes slow?

_____

9   Temperatures today are forecast to reach 102°F. It is 85°F now. How many degrees will the temperature increase if the forecast is accurate?

_____

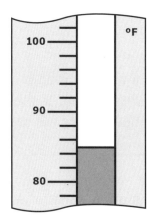

10   If the temperature on the thermometer falls 9 degrees from the current temperature, what will the temperature be?

_____

☆   **Tell how you solved Problem 7. How do you know your answer is reasonable?**

Name _____ **Date** _____

Solve.

1 7.25 h – 4 h 15 min = _____ min

2 50 mi – 5,000 yd = _____ yd

3 1,700 lb x 5 = _____ t

4 6 lb 8 oz – 20 oz = ___ lb ___ oz

5 20 yd ÷ 16 = _____ in.

6 67°C – 39°C = _____ °C

---

7 What is the length of the trail in meters?

_____

Trail start

Trail end

SCALE
1 cm = 150 m

---

8 The diagram shows the distance between Corpus Christi and San Antonio. Driving at an average of 50 miles per hour, how many hours would it take to get from one city to the other? Use the ruler to measure.

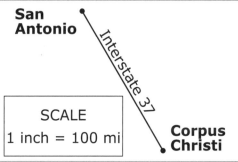

San Antonio

Interstate 37

SCALE
1 inch = 100 mi

Corpus Christi

---

9 Mrs. Kim buys food on her shopping list in the amounts shown. If she places everything in one bag, how heavy will the bag be in ounces?

_____

Shopping List
apples – 3.3 lbs.
cherries – 18 oz
eggplant – 1.5 lbs.
beans (can) – 15 oz
garlic – 6 oz

10 Beans are 3 cans for $2.00. If Mrs. Kim buys $4.00 worth of beans, how many pounds of beans does she buy?

_____

 Tell how you solved Problem 9. How do you know your answer is reasonable?

Name _____ **Date** _____

Solve.

1 Sara gets to school at 8:35 A.M. She leaves school at 2:40 P.M. and then spends $1\frac{1}{2}$ hours at the library. What time is it when she leaves the library? How many hours did Sara spend at school and library together?

2 Adrian's house has a 30-gallon water heater. He has 3 children. If each of his children takes a bath using 20 quarts of hot water, how many gallons of hot water are left for his shower?

3 The driving distance from Amarillo to Abilene is 280 miles. Driving at an average of 45 miles per hour, how many hours would it take to get from one city to the other?

4 The couch is 3 meters long. The length of the living room wall between the two windows is 4 meters. If the couch is centered on the wall between the two windows, how many centimeters of empty wall space will be on either side?

5 The current temperature is 65°F. The forecast says the high temperature for the day will be 82°F. How many degrees will the temperature increase if the forecast is accurate?

6 Rafi bought 1 1/2 pounds of apples, 16 ounces of blueberries, 8 ounces of raspberries, 14 ounces of blackberries, 10 ounces of kiwi, 1/2 pound of grapes, and 2 pounds of watermelon to make a fruit salad. How many pounds of fruit did he buy?

Circle the letter for the correct answer.

7 On average, the human eye blinks once every 5 seconds. About how many times does the eye blink in 1 hour?

    A 12

    B 72

    C 300

    D 720

8 The tea factory has 3 tons of dried tea leaves ready to be packaged. If each box of tea contains 8 ounces of tea leaves, how many boxes can be filled?

    A 12,000

    B 1,200

    C 2,400

    D 24,000

Unit 25 Mini-Lesson ★

Estimate Perimeter and Circumference

Standard

IV. Measurement

6.8A (SS) Estimate measurements (including circumference) and evaluate reasonableness of results.

6.8B (RS) Select and use appropriate units, tools, or formulas to measure and to solve problems involving length (including perimeter), area, time, temperature, volume, and weight.

Model the Skill

Draw the following figures on the board.

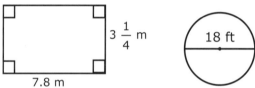

◆ **Say: Perimeter** *is the distance around the outside of a figure with vertices.* **Circumference** *is the distance around a circle. We can estimate the perimeter of a figure by rounding the measurements and applying an appropriate formula.*

◆ **Ask:** *What is 7.8 rounded to the nearest whole number?* (8) *What is 3 1/4 rounded to the nearest whole number?* (3) Write the formula $P = 2l + 2w$ on the board and guide students in estimating the perimeter with the rounded numbers. (*P* is about 22 m)

◆ **Say:** *To estimate the distance around a circle, we use the relationship of the diameter to the circumference.* Review circle relationships in Unit 20 if necessary, reminding students that the circumference is about 3 times the length of the diameter.

◆ **Ask:** *What is 18 rounded to the nearest ten?* (20) *What should I do next to estimate the circumference?* (multiply by 3) *About how long is the circumference?* (about 60 ft)

◆ Assign students the appropriate practice page(s) to support their understanding of the skill.

Assess the Skill

Use the following problems to pre-/post-assess students' understanding of the skill.

Perimeter is about _____   Circumference is about _____

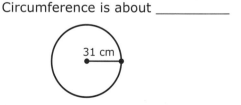

STAAR Mathematics Practice Grade 6 • ©2013 Newmark Learning, LLC

Name _____ **Date** _____

Complete the chart.

	Figure	Round numbers	Formula	Estimate
1	56 cm 56 cm	56 ⟶ ☐ rounds to	$P = 4s$ $P = 4 \times$ ____	*P is about* ____
2	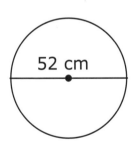 4.5 m 6 m 3.2 m	4.5 ⟶ ☐ 3.2 ⟶ ☐ 6 ⟶ ☐	$P = s + s + s$	*P is about* ____
3	19 ft $12\frac{1}{3}$ ft	$12\frac{1}{3}$ ⟶ ☐ 19 ⟶ ☐	$P = 2l + 2w$	*P is about* ____

Estimate each circumference.

4

52 cm

52 $\xrightarrow{\text{rounds to}}$ ☐

____ × 3 = ____

Circumference is about ____

5

$5\frac{1}{4}$ ft

$5\frac{1}{4}$ ⟶ ☐

____ × 3 = ____

Circumference is about ____

 Tell why we use rounded numbers to estimate.

Name _____ **Date** _____

Estimate each perimeter or circumference. Show your work.

❶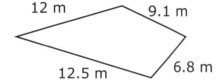

12 m   9.1 m

12.5 m   6.8 m

12.5 $\xrightarrow{\text{rounds to}}$ _____
6.8 $\longrightarrow$ _____
9.1 $\longrightarrow$ _____
12 $\longrightarrow$ _____
Perimeter is about _____

❷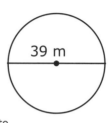

39 m

39 $\xrightarrow{\text{rounds to}}$ _____
____ x 3 = ____
Circumference is about ____

❸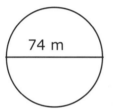

74 m

Circumference is about ____

❹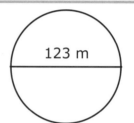

123 m

Circumference is about ____

❺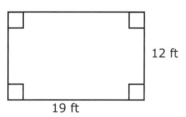

12 ft

19 ft

Perimeter is about ____

❻

306 m

97 m

Perimeter is about ____

❼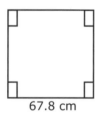

67.8 cm

Perimeter is about ____

❽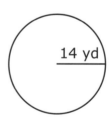

14 yd

Perimeter is about ____

 Tell why we multiply the diameter by 3 to estimate circumference.

Name _____ **Date** _____

Solve.

1 The perimeter of a square room is about 52 feet. About how long is one side of the room?

2 The circumference of a circular mirror is about 1 meter. About how long is the diameter of the mirror in centimeters?

---

3 Use a ruler to measure the figure to the nearest $\frac{1}{2}$ inch. Then estimate the perimeter.

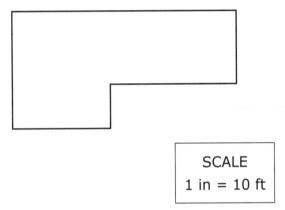

SCALE
1 in = 10 ft

Circle the letter for the correct answer.

4 Which is the best estimate for the circumference of the circle below?

5.8 m

A about 12 m

B about 15 m

C about 18 m

D about 36 m

5 Which is the best estimate for the perimeter of the figure below?

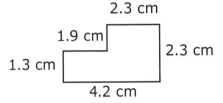

2.3 cm

1.9 cm

1.3 cm

2.3 cm

4.2 cm

A about 12 cm

B about 9 cm

C about 18 cm

D about 15 cm

Unit 26 Mini-Lesson ★
Estimate and Find Area

Standard

IV. Measurement

6.8A (SS) Estimate measurements (including circumference) and evaluate reasonableness of results.

6.8B (RS) Select and use appropriate units, tools, or formulas to measure and to solve problems involving length (including perimeter), area, time, temperature, volume, and weight.

Model the Skill

Draw the following figures on the board.

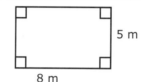 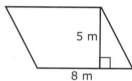

◆ **Ask:** *What is area?* (The number of square units in a region) *How do we find the area of a rectangle?* (multiply length times width) Write the formula, $A = l \times w$, below the rectangle and have a volunteer find the area of the rectangle. Then draw a diagonal on the rectangle, forming 2 triangles.

◆ **Ask:** *How can you describe the area of this triangle?* (half the area of the rectangle) Point out that the formula for the area of a triangle shows just that. Draw a triangle and label base and height. Write the formula $A = 1/2 \ b \times h$.

◆ **Say:** *Look at the parallelogram. We can find its area by multiplying the base times height just as we can do for the rectangle. Why?* Guide students to understand that length and width in a rectangle represents the same relationship as base and height in a parallelogram. Write the formula $A = b \times h$ below the rectangle and the parallelogram. Allow students to explore cutting a triangle from a parallelogram and moving it to create a rectangle with the same area.

◆ Assign students the appropriate practice page(s) to support their understanding of the skill.

Assess the Skill

Use the following problems to pre-/post-assess students' understanding of the skill.

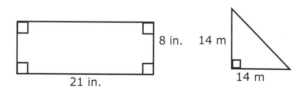 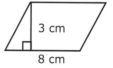

Area = _____   Area = _____   Area = _____

Name _____ **Date** _____

Complete the chart.

	Figure	Formula	Estimate
1	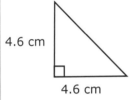	$A = l \cdot w$ or $A = b \cdot h$	$A =$ _____ ft²
2	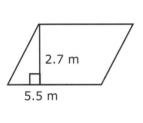	$A = \frac{1}{2}b \cdot h$ $A = \frac{b \cdot h}{2}$	$A =$ _____ cm²
3	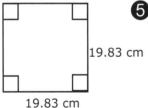	$A = b \cdot h$	$A =$ _____

Estimate the area of each figure. Round measurements to the nearest whole number.

4 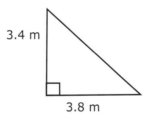   **5** 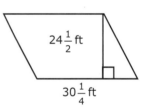   **6**

19.83 ⟶ _____   3.4 ⟶ _____

A = _____   3.8 ⟶ _____ $24\frac{1}{2}$ ⟶ _____

                          A = _____ $30\frac{1}{4}$ ⟶ _____

                                                    A = _____

  Tell what the base and height of a rectangle mean.

Name _____ Date _____

Choose the best estimate for the area of each figure.

1 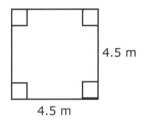 4.5 m

4.5 m

Area is about

_____

2 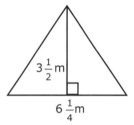 $3\frac{1}{2}$ m

$6\frac{1}{4}$ m

Area is about

_____

Estimates
21 m²
18 m²
28 m²
25 m²
12 m²

3 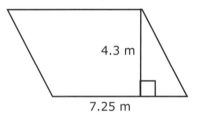 4.3 m

7.25 m

Area is about

_____

4 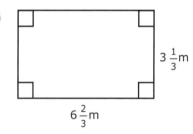 $3\frac{1}{3}$ m

$6\frac{2}{3}$ m

Area is about

_____

Estimate the area of each figure.

5 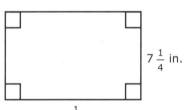 $7\frac{1}{4}$ in.

$10\frac{1}{2}$ in.

Area = _____

6 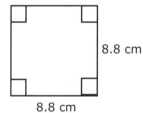 8.8 cm

8.8 cm

Area = _____

7 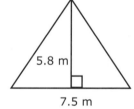 5.8 m

7.5 m

Area = _____

8 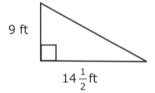 9 ft

$14\frac{1}{2}$ ft

Area = _____

9 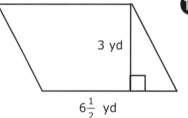 3 yd

$6\frac{1}{2}$ yd

Area = _____

10 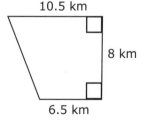 10.5 km

8 km

6.5 km

Area = _____

⭐ **Tell why the area of a triangle is $\frac{1}{2}$ the area of a parallelogram.**

 STAAR Mathematics Practice Grade 6 • ©2013 Newmark Learning, LLC

Name _____ **Date** _____

Solve.

1 Mrs. Orlando wants to carpet the floor of a rectangular room that is 14 feet long and 12 feet wide. How many square feet of carpet does she need to cover the floor?

2 Felix bought a new sail for his sailboat. The sail is a right triangle that has a height of 25 feet and base of 12 feet. About how many square yards of sailcloth were used to make the sail?

---

3 Find the area of the triangle below.

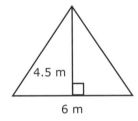

4 Estimate the area of the parallelogram below.

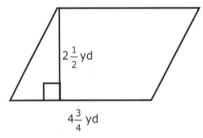

---

5 Estimate the area of a window that has a height of 64 inches and a width of 48 inches.

6 Find the area of a scalene triangle that has a height of 35 cm and a base of 72 cm.

Circle the letter for the correct answer.

7 Which is the best estimate for the area of the triangle?

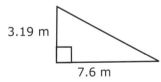

A 12 m²

B 21 m²

C 24 m²

D 28 m²

8 Which is the best estimate for the area of the quadrilateral?

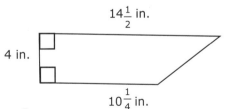

A 60 in.²

B 40 in.²

C 30 in.²

D 50 in.²

Unit 27 Mini-Lesson ★
Estimate and Find Volume

Standard

IV. Measurement

6.8A (SS) Estimate measurements (including circumference) and evaluate reasonableness of results.

6.8B (RS) Select and use appropriate units, tools, or formulas to measure and to solve problems involving length (including perimeter), area, time, temperature, volume, and weight.

Model the Skill

◆ **Say:** *We can find the volume of different solid or three-dimensional shapes in different ways. Today we are going to use formulas to find the volume of cubes and other rectangular prisms.*

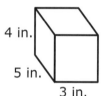

$$V = l \times w \times h$$
or
$$V = \text{Area of base} \times h$$

◆ **Say:** *Use the formula to find the volume of this rectangular prism. Remember, when we multiply to find the area, we multiply the unit x unit (unit²), so we show our answer in square units. When we multiply to find volume, we multiply unit x unit x unit (unit³) so therefore we show our answer in cubic units. What is the volume?* (60 cubic inches)

◆ Assign students the appropriate practice page(s) to support their understanding of the skill.

Assess the Skill

Use the following problems to pre-/post-assess students' understanding of the skill.

◆ Ask students to calculate the volume of these figures.

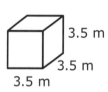

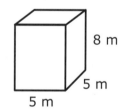

Name _____ Date _____

Use the formula *V = bh* or *V = l* x *w* x *h* to find the volume of each.

1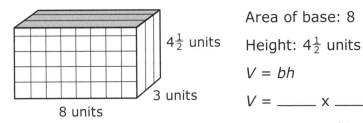

$4\frac{1}{2}$ units

3 units

8 units

Area of base: 8 x 3 = _____ square units

Height: $4\frac{1}{2}$ units

$V = bh$

$V = $ _____ x _____

$V = $ _____ cubic units

2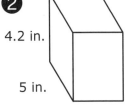

4.2 in.

5 in.

3.6 in.

$V = l$ x w x h

$V = bh$

$V = $ _____ x _____ x _____

$V = $ _____ cubic inches

3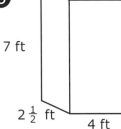

7 ft

$2\frac{1}{2}$ ft

4 ft

$V = $ _____

4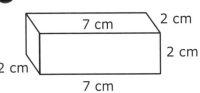

7 cm

2 cm

2 cm

2 cm

7 cm

$V = $ _____

5

3 m

$6\frac{1}{2}$ m

3 m

5 m

$V = $ _____

6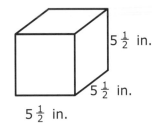

$5\frac{1}{2}$ in.

$5\frac{1}{2}$ in.

$5\frac{1}{2}$ in.

$V = $ _____

---

7 A rectangular box
9.7 feet long, 6 feet wide,
and 4 feet high

$V = $ _____ cubic feet

8 A cube
$7\frac{1}{2}$ inches long

$V = $ _____ cubic inches

9 A rectangular box
11 feet long, 3 feet wide,
and $5\frac{1}{2}$ feet high

$V = $ _____ cubic feet

☆ **Tell which formula for finding volume you prefer to use. Tell why.**

Name _____ Date _____

Use the formula $V = bh$ or $V = l \times w \times h$ to find the volume of each.

1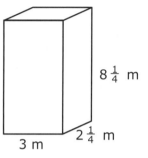

$V = $ _____

2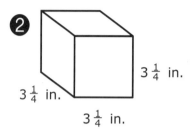

$V = $ _____

3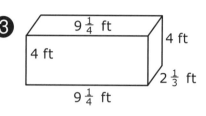

$V = $ _____

4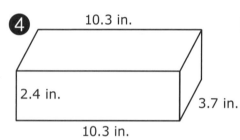

$V = $ _____

5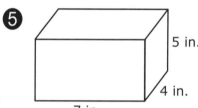

$V = $ _____

6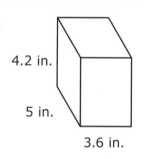

$V = $ _____

7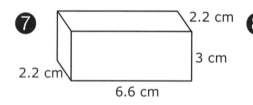

$V = $ _____

8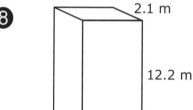

$V = $ _____

9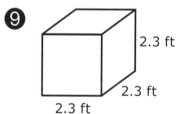

$V = $ _____

10 A rectangular box 12.7 cm long, 7.1 cm wide, and 3 cm high

$V = $ _____ cubic cm

11 A cube $11\frac{1}{4}$ inches long

$V = $ _____ cubic inches

12 A rectangular box 9.8 feet long, 4 feet wide, and $2\frac{1}{2}$ feet high

$V = $ _____ cubic feet

 Look at Problem 5. How would you change the dimensions of the box to double the volume? Explain.

STAAR Mathematics Practice Grade 6 • ©2013 Newmark Learning, LLC

Name _____ **Date** _____

Solve.

1 A locker is 1 foot long, 1 foot wide, and $4\frac{1}{4}$ feet high. What is the volume of the locker?

2 The refrigerator came in a box that was 6 feet high, 3 feet wide, and $3\frac{1}{2}$ feet deep. What was the volume of the box?

3 A pizza box is 2 inches high, $16\frac{3}{4}$ inches wide, and $16\frac{3}{4}$ inches long. What is the volume of the pizza box?

4 The feeding trough is 4 meters long, 0.5 meters wide, and 0.25 meters high. What is the volume of the trough?

5 The fish tank is 40 centimeters wide, 100 centimeters long, and 60 centimeters deep. If 1 cubic centimeter is equal to 1 milliliter, how many milliliters of water will we need to fill the tank?

6 The reflection pool is 1 meter deep, 10 meters wide, and 20.5 meters long. What is the volume of the pool?

Circle the letter for the best answer.

7 A moving company sells boxes for packing. What is the volume of the box below?

A 360 cubic in.

B 370 cubic in.

C 380 cubic in.

D 3,600 cubic in.

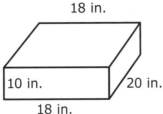

18 in.

10 in.   20 in.

18 in.

8 The suitcase is 50 centimeters long, 35 centimeters wide, and 20 centimeters deep. What is the volume of the suitcase?

A 350 cubic cm

B 3,500 cubic cm

C 35,000 cubic cm

D 350,000 cubic cm

Unit 28 Mini-Lesson ★
Use Lists and Tree Diagrams

Standard

V. Probability and Statistics

6.9A (SS) Construct sample spaces using lists and tree diagrams.

Model the Skill

Draw two spinners on the board.

- ◆ **Ask:** *What are all the possible outcomes of spinning the first spinner one time?* (ABCDE) *How many possible outcomes is that?* (5) List the outcomes on the board. *What are all the possible outcomes of spinning the second spinner one time?* (red, blue) *How many possible outcomes is that?* (2)

- ◆ **Ask:** *What if we spin the first spinner and then the second spinner? How can we can show the outcomes from two different experiments?* Discuss how to write an organized list: red A, red B, . . . blue A, blue B, . . .

- ◆ **Say:** *Another way to show the outcomes from two different experiments, or* **compound event**, *is to make a tree diagram.* Construct a tree diagram on the board.

- ◆ **Ask:** *How many possible outcomes does the tree diagram show?* (10) Guide students to see that the number of possible outcomes listed for each spinner, when multiplied together, gives the number of possible outcomes shown by the tree diagram.

- ◆ Assign students the appropriate practice page(s) to support their understanding of the skill.

Assess the Skill

Use the following problems to pre-/post-assess students' understanding of the skill.

Have students list all the possible outcomes of each experiment, then make a tree diagram to show the outcomes for doing both experiments one time.

Tossing a number cube, each face labeled 1, 2, 3, 4, 5, 6

Tossing a coin

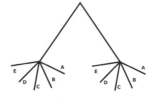

STAAR Mathematics Practice Grade 6 • ©2013 Newmark Learning, LLC

Name _____ Date _____

Make a list for each.

1 What are the possible outcomes of spinning spinner I once?

_____

2 What are the possible outcomes of spinning spinner II once?

_____

3 What are all the possible outcomes of spinning spinner I and spinner II one time?

A1, A2, _____, _____, B1, _____, _____, _____

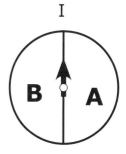

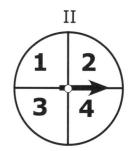

Complete the tree diagram for each compound event.

4 Spinning Spinner I and Spinner II once.

What is the number of total outcomes?

_____

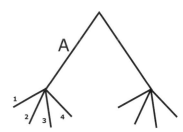

5 Tossing a coin twice.

What is the number of total possible outcomes?

_____

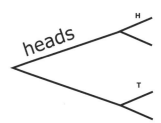

6 Showing the results of choosing at random among 3 sandwiches (tuna, egg, or cheese), and 2 fruits (apple or pear).

What is the number of total possible outcomes?

_____

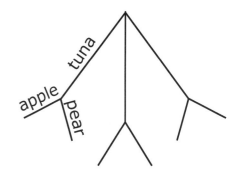

 Tell what a compound event is.

Name _____ Date _____

Make a list for each.

1 A number cube has the numbers 1–6 on its faces. What are the potential outcomes of tossing the number cube once?

_____

2 What are the outcomes of spinning the spinner once?

_____

3 What are all the possible outcomes of tossing the number cube and spinning the spinner one time?

_____

4 Without making a list, how can you tell how many outcomes are possible if the number cube is tossed twice?

_____

Make a tree diagram for each compound event.

5 Rolling a number cube numbered 1–6 twice. What is the number of total outcomes?

_____

6 Spinning a spinner twice on a color wheel with the primary colors red, blue, and yellow. What is the number of total possible outcomes?

_____

7 Showing the results of a person choosing at random among 4 breakfasts: pancakes, waffles, french toast, or cereal, and two juices: orange or apple. What is the number of total possible outcomes?

_____

☆ **Tell the ways you can find the number of total possible outcomes for a compound event.**

Name _____ Date _____

Solve.

1 A bag of bows for gift wrapping has large and small bows in gold, silver, red, white, and blue. Make a tree diagram to show all possible outcomes of picking one bow at random.

2 A triangular pyramid with sides numbered 1–4 is tossed 3 times. Make a tree diagram to show all possible outcomes.

Circle the letter for the correct answer.

3 Which tree diagram shows the possible outcomes of a coin being tossed twice? Show the possible outcomes

A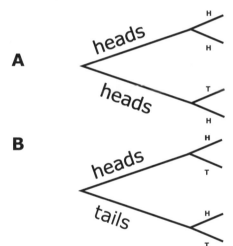

B

C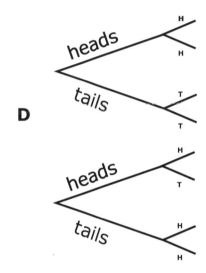

D

4 Which is NOT a possible outcome if you spin the spinners below one time?

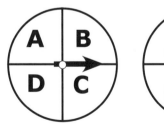 

A A ◯

B ◯ ▢

C D △

D D ▱

Unit 29 Mini-Lesson ★
Find Probability

Standard

V. Probability and Statistics

6.9B (SS) Find probabilities of a simple event and its complement and describe the relationship between the two.

Model the Skill

Draw this spinner on the board.

◆ **Say:** *We find the probability of an event by writing a ratio. Remember how we listed all the outcomes of an experiment?* Write *P* (*E*) = the number of favorable outcomes/number of possible outcomes on the board.

◆ **Ask:** *What are the possible outcomes of the spinner on the board?* (QRST) *How many possible outcomes are there?* (4)

◆ **Ask:** *So if Q is the outcome we want, or the favorable outcome, what is the probability of the spinner stopping on Q?* (1:4) As you write P (Q) = $\frac{1}{4}$, *read the equation, the probability of Q is 1 out of 4, or one-fourth.*

◆ **Ask:** *What is the probability of the spinner stopping on Q, R, S, or T?* ($\frac{4}{4}$ or 1)

◆ *What is the probability of the spinner NOT landing on Q?* ($\frac{3}{4}$) Discuss the idea that the probability of an event occurring falls between 0, impossible to happen, and 1, certain to happen. So if *P* (*Q*) = $\frac{1}{4}$, then *P* (not *Q*) = $\frac{3}{4}$. Think $1 - \frac{1}{4}$.

◆ Assign students the appropriate practice page(s) to support their understanding of the skill.

Assess the Skill

Use the following problems to pre-/post-assess students' understanding of the skill.

Have students find the probability for each event.

   P (4) = _____   *P* (not 4) _____

   P (*H*) = _____   *P* (not *H*) _____

STAAR Mathematics Practice Grade 6 • ©2013 Newmark Learning, LLC

Name _____ **Date** _____

Solve.

1 What are the outcomes of spinning the spinner once?

_____

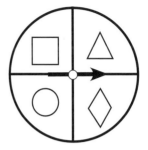

2 How many possible outcome are there?

_____

3 What is the probability of the spinner stopping on △?

$P(\triangle) =$ _____

4 What is the probability of the spinner stopping on ☐ ?

$P(\square) =$ _____

5 What is the probability of the spinner NOT stopping on ☐ ?

$P(\text{not } \square) =$ _____

A number cube has the numbers 1–6 on its faces.
If the number cube is tossed once, what is the probability of:

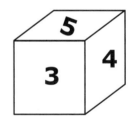

6 tossing 1?

$P(1) =$ _____

7 tossing 4?

$P(4) =$ _____

8 NOT tossing 5?

$P(\text{not } 5) =$ _____

9 tossing an odd number?

$P(\text{odd number}) =$ _____

10 tossing an even number?

$P(\text{even number}) =$ _____

11 tossing a number less than 3?

$P(\text{number less than 3}) =$ _____

 Tell what number represents a certain event. Explain.

Name _____ Date _____

Use the spinner to find the probability for each event.

1 *P* (9) _____

2 *P* (even number) _____

3 *P* (composite number) _____

4 *P* (divisible by 3) _____

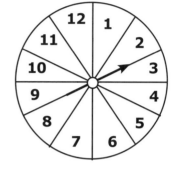

5 *P* (2-digit number) _____

6 *P* (factor of 10) _____

7 *P* (1-digit number) _____

8 *P* (not divisible by 6) _____

Solve.

9 A bag is filled with 20 donuts. If a donut is selected at random, the probability of choosing a jelly donut is $\frac{7}{20}$. How many donuts in the bag are jelly donuts? How many are not jelly donuts? _____

10 Sofia picks a card on the right without looking. What is the probability that she will pick the star? _____

11 What is the probability that Sofia will pick a fruit? _____

12 Riley has 4 books to read this vacation. One is a realistic fiction novel, one is a historical novel, one is a sci-fi adventure, and one is a nonfiction book about space exploration. If he reads them in any order, what is the probability that he will read a nonfiction book first?

13 What is the probability that he will read a fiction book first?

 If the probability of rain is $\frac{2}{3}$, tell what the probability is of no rain. Why?

Name _____ Date _____

Solve. Use the spinner for Problems 1–4.

1 What is the probability that the spinner will stop on an even number?

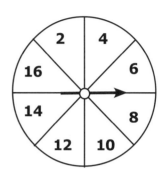

2 What is the probability that the spinner will stop on a prime number?

3 What is the probability that the spinner will stop on a 1-digit number?

4 What is the probability that the spinner will stop on a 2-digit number twice in a row?

Circle the letter for the correct answer.

5 Dan downloads 15 songs on his phone. Seven songs are country music and the rest are hip-hop. If Dan plays a song at random, which expression represents the probability that the song he plays will be hip-hop?

A $1 + \frac{7}{15}$

B $1 + \frac{8}{15}$

C $1 - \frac{8}{15}$

D $1 - \frac{7}{15}$

6 If Dan's phone plays music in a random shuffle and never plays the same song twice in a row, which expression represents the probability that the phone will play 2 different country songs in a row?

A $\frac{7}{15} + \frac{6}{15}$

B $\frac{7}{15} \times \frac{6}{15}$

C $\frac{8}{15} - \frac{7}{15}$

D $\frac{7}{15} \div \frac{6}{15}$

Unit 30 Mini-Lesson ★
Find Mean, Median, and Mode

Standard

V. Probability & Statistics

6.10B (SS) Identify mean ([using concrete objects and] pictorial models), median, mode, and range of a set of data.

Model the Skill

Write the following definitions on the board, followed by the data set below.

Mean: the average; the sum of all the data divided by the number of data

Median: the middle number in an ordered set of data

Mode: the number that occurs most often in a set of data (there can be more than one mode or no mode)

◆ **Say:** *Today we are going to be finding the mean, median, and mode for different data sets. What is the mean?* (The mean is the sum of all the data, divided by the number of data.)

◆ Assign students the appropriate practice page(s) to support their understanding of the skill. Remind students to check and recheck their work.

Assess the Skill

Use the following problems to pre-/post-assess students' understanding of the skill.

◆ Ask students to find the mean, mode, and median for the following data sets:

$50, $35, $50, $25, $30   130, 142, 134, 140, 134, 133, 135

STAAR Mathematics Practice Grade 6 • ©2013 Newmark Learning, LLC

Name _____ Date _____

> **Mean (average):** the sum of all the data divided by the number of the data
> **Median:** the middle number in a set of data when the data are arranged in order
> **Mode:** the number that occurs most often in a set of data (there can be more than one mode or no mode)

Find the mean, median, or mode for each data set.

1 Weekly earnings of 5 dog walkers:
$48, $35, $50, $27, $25

(____ + ____ + ____ + ____ + ____) ÷ ____

Mean = $_____

$25, ____, ____, ____, ____

Median = $_____

> Think: Order the data to find the middle number.

2 Monthly rainfall (in inches):
1, 0, 3, 0.5, 0.5, 1

Mean = _____

Median = _____

> Remember: When there are two middle numbers, the median is the average of the two.

3 Annual snowfall (in inches):
20, 16, 20, 17.5, 19.5, 18, 23

Mean = _____   Median = _____

4 Foreign-language class sizes (students):
21, 20, 24, 22, 22, 22, 16

Mean = _____   Median = _____

5 Math test scores (in points):
100, 90, 72, 95, 85, 83, 89, 81, 86, 93, 98

Mean = _____   Median = _____

6 Goals per soccer game:
4, 3, 1, 1, 2, 2, 3, 3, 2

Mean = _____   Median = _____

7 Daily low temperatures (°F):
19, 20, 18, 19, 17, 30, 17, 19

Mode(s) = _____

8 Marathon times (in hours):
3.0, 3.5, 3.75, 4.25, 4.0, 3.75, 4.25, 4.5

Mode(s) = _____

9 Weekly babysitting earnings:
$25, $20, $25, $35, $27, $30

Mean = _____
Median = _____
Mode(s) = _____

10 Monthly electric bill:
$195, $207, $203, $245, $237, $211

Mean = _____
Median = _____
Mode(s) = _____

☆ **A newspaper reports the median house price is $250,000. From that standard, tell what you know about housing prices.**

Name _____ Date _____

Use the report on the right to find the mean, median, and mode of the test scores for each student.

1 Scott

Mean = _____

Median = _____

Mode = _____

Math Test Scores Report

Scott: 75, 52, 80, 88, 100

Olivia: 98, 92, 88, 92, 95

Gemma: 84, 92, 85, 73, 86

Chris: 88, 86, 93, 88, 90

2 Olivia

Mean = _____

Median = _____

Mode = _____

3 Gemma

Mean = _____

Median = _____

Mode = _____

4 Chris

Mean = _____

Median = _____

Mode = _____

Find the mean, median, and mode for each data set.

5 Monthly rainfall (in inches):
1, 0, 2, 0.5, 0.25, 3, 0.25

Mean = _____ Median = _____

Mode(s) = _____

6 July 4th temperatures (°F):
89, 94, 96, 99, 96, 97, 95, 92

Mean = _____ Median = _____

Mode(s) = _____

7 Baby sleep log (in hours):
10, 8, 9, 8, 8.25, 9.25, 8.5

Mean = _____ Median = _____

Mode(s) = _____

8 Daily running log (in kilometers):
3.5, 0, 2.5, 5, 2.5, 3, 4.5

Mean = _____ Median = _____

Mode(s) = _____

9 Reading log (in pages):
21, 42, 25, 45, 37, 34, 30

Mean = _____ Median = _____

Mode(s) = _____

10 Monthly snowfall (in inches):
0.5, 2, 5, 0.25, 1

Mean = _____ Median = _____

Mode(s) = _____

☆ **Look at your answers for Problems 1–4. Which measure best describes the students' test scores? Explain.** _____

_____

Name _____ **Date** _____

Solve.

1 Sanjay has 6 math test scores. They are 83, 80, 88, 86, 88, 70. What is the median score?

2 For the first week of December, the daily low temperatures (°F) were 36, 40, 38, 41, 40, 32, 34. What was the mode?

3 Rachel ran 5 miles every day last week. Her running time was as follows: 39 min, 42 min, 41 min, 38 min, 39 min, 39 min, 42 min. What was her mean running time for 5 miles?

4 Ms. Krill's ten honor students scored the following grades on the pop quiz: 83, 90, 98, 96, 88, 98, 95, 97, 98, 100. What is the mode score?

5 On the bike trip, we rode 10 kilometers on Day 1, 18 kilometers on Day 2, 20 kilometers on Day 3, 15 kilometers on Day 4, and 18 kilometers on Day 5. What was the median distance we rode?

6 The rainfall for the second week in April was as follows (in inches): 1, 0, 2.5, 0.4, 0.8, 3, 0. What was the mean daily rainfall that week?

Circle the letter for the correct answer.

7 What is the mean of the data set 20, 12, 18, 25, 20?

    A 20

    B 19

    C 18

    D 13

8 What is the mean of the data set 112, 120, 114, 113, 118, 115, 113?

    A 113

    B 114

    C 115

    D 120

Unit 31 Mini-Lesson ★

Make and Interpret Dot Plots

Standard

V. Probability & Statistics

6.10B (SS), 6.10D (RS) Identify mean ([using concrete objects and] pictorial models), median, mode, and range of a set of data; Solve problems by collecting, organizing, displaying, and interpreting data.

Model the Skill

◆ **Say:** *Today we are using data to make dot plots. A dot plot is like a line plot, but with dots instead of X's. Look at the data.* Explain how you could show this information. Draw the following dot plot and data on the board.

<table>
<tr><td>Class Survey</td></tr>
<tr><td>How many sports do you play?</td></tr>
<tr><td>0, 2, 1, 3, 1, 2, 0, 3, 2,</td></tr>
<tr><td>2, 1, 2, 1, 0, 2, 1</td></tr>
</table>

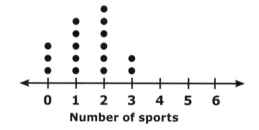

Number of sports

◆ Guide students to use the data to complete the dot plot. **Ask:** How is it useful to represent data in this way? (Shows results in a clear, organized, visual way)

◆ Assign students the appropriate practice page(s) to support their understanding of the skill.

Assess the Skill

Use the following problems to pre-/post-assess students' understanding of the skill.

◆ Ask students to conduct their own class survey asking questions such as shoe size, height, number of siblings, etc., and then use their survey result data to make a dot plot.

Name _____ Date _____

Use the dot plot to answer each question.

1 How many students participated in the survey? _____

Think: Each dot represents one student.

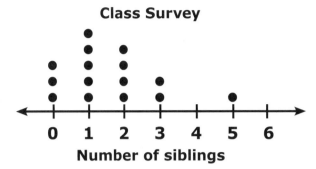

2 What is the range of the data? _____

Think: Subtract the least number from the greatest number (5–0). The difference is the range.

3 What is the mode of the data? _____

4 What is the median of the data? _____

Use the data to make a dot plot. Then answer each question.

5

Class Survey
How many sports do you play?
3, 2, 3, 4, 4, 1, 0, 2, 2, 3, 0, 2, 1, 4, 2

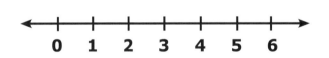

6 How many dots should you place above 3 on the number line? _____

7 What number occurs most frequently? _____

8 How many students participated in the survey? _____

9 What is the mean of the data? _____

 Look at Problem 4. Tell how you found the median. Use the median to make a statement about the data: "The survey shows . . ."

Name _____ Date _____

Use the dot plot to answer each question.

1 What is the range of the data?

_____

2 What is the median of the data?

_____

3 What is the mode of the data?

_____

4 Of the three measures above, which describes the data best? Why?

_____

Survey of 10 School Students

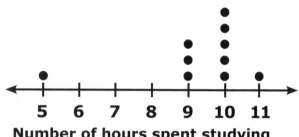

Number of hours spent studying each week

Use the data to make a line plot. Then answer each question.

Class Survey

How many hours do you study?

6, 2, 5, 4, 4, 1, 2, 2,

3, 5, 2, 1, 5, 2

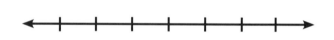

5 What number occurs most frequently?

_____

6 What is the mode of the data? _____

7 What is the mean of the data? _____

8 What is the range of the data? _____

9 What is the median of the data?

_____

10 Of the measures above, which describes the data best? Why?

_____

_____

 What is the average number of hours spent studying according to the survey data at the top of the page? Explain how you found the mean.

_____

_____

Name _____ Date _____

Solve. Use the dot plot.

1 What is the range of scores on Sam's math quizzes? _____

2 What is the mode? _____

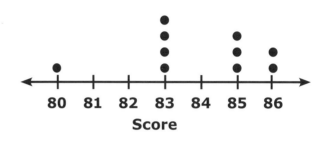

Sam's Math Quiz Scores

Score

3 What is the median score? _____

4 What is the mean household size on Cedar Circle? _____

5 What are the modes? _____

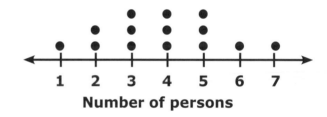

Cedar Circle Household Size

Number of persons

6 What is the median? _____

Circle the letter for the correct answer.

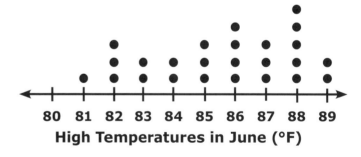

7 Which statement is true based on the data in the line plot?

Class size at Kennedy School

A Class size ranges from 22 to 31.

B Half of the classes have 26 students.

C The most common class size is 28.

D The median class size is 25.

8 Which statement is false based on the data in the line plot?

High Temperatures in June (°F)

A The temperature in June ranges from 80 to 89.

B The least common temperature in June is 81.

C The most common high temperature is 88.

D The median temperature is 86.

Unit 32 Mini-Lesson ★
Make and Interpret Stem and Leaf Plots

Standard

V. Probability and Statistics

6.10B (SS) Identify mean ([using concrete objects and] pictorial models), median, mode, and range of a set of data.

6.10D (RS) Solve problems by collecting, organizing, displaying, and interpreting data.

Model the Skill

Write the following data and draw a stem and leaf plot on the board.

Stem	Leaf
1	7 8 8 9
	9 9
2	

Wellness Clinic
Baby weight at 12 months (lb)
17, 19, 20, 18, 18, 21, 19, 23, 21, 19, 22

◆ **Say:** *Today we are going to use place value to create a stem and leaf plot. Here is some data from a health clinic about the weight of babies that the doctors saw one day.*

◆ **Ask:** *What does the stem represent?* (represents ten; the data has 2 digits) *What does the leaf represent?* (ones) *What number is 1 | 9?* (19)

◆ **Ask:** *What should we write for leaves for the stem 2?* (0, 1, 1, 2, 3) *What number is 2 | 0?* (20) Point out that the data is displayed in order by place value and from least to greatest, the last digit of the number being the leaf.

◆ **Say:** *It is easy to see the range of data, and the mode. We have to count to find the median.* Have students look at the plot and tell range (23 – 17 = 6), mode (19), and median (19), then interpret the data with those measures.

◆ Assign students the appropriate practice page(s) to support their understanding of the skill.

Assess the Skill

Use the following problems to pre-/post-assess students' understanding of the skill.

Have students create a stem and leaf plot with the following data, then tell range, median, and mode.

Test Scores
93, 90, 72, 85, 67, 85, 90, 98, 88, 87, 90, 75, 78, 89, 95

Name _____ **Date** _____

Use the data to complete each stem and leaf plot. Then answer each question.

  1

Points Scored				
TEAM RED				
34	12	15	28	7
15	22	25	15	30
12	27	26	32	15

Stem	Leaf
0	7
1	2 2 5
2	

2 How many points did Team Red score most often?

_____

3 Did Team Red usually score more than 22 points? Explain.

_____

4

Cookie Sales by Store			
Number of Boxes Sold in One Week			
205	215	217	209
220	216	225	207
213	220	223	

Stem	Leaf
20	5
21	
22	

5 How many stores are there?

_____

6 What is the most common number of boxes sold?

_____

7 Which sales figures are in the bottom half?

_____

8 What is the range in sales?

_____

 ☆ **Tell how you organize data in a stem and leaf plot.**

Name _____ Date _____

Display the data in a stem and leaf plot. Then answer each question.

1

Mr. B's Math Class Final Exam Test Scores				
85	90	82	85	100
95	78	70	100	98
92	85	99		

Stem	Leaf

2 How many students took the exam?

_____

3 What is the range in test scores?

_____

4 What score was achieved by the greatest number of students? _____

5 How many students scored above the median score? _____

6 If the average score is 89, how many students scored above average?

_____

7

Mary Jo's Bagel Shop				
SUNDAY'S ORDERS, 6 A.M. – 7 A.M.				
12	6	12	13	18
24	6	6	12	12
12	13	12	8	6
12	8	6	10	24

Stem	Leaf

8 How many orders did the bagel shop get on Sunday between 6 and 7 A.M.?

_____

9 Which amount represents the mode?

_____

10 How many orders were greater than a dozen?

_____

11 What was the range of the orders?

_____

☆ **Tell how you find median and mode on a stem and leaf plot.**

Name _____ **Date** _____

Solve.

1 What is the range, median, and mode of the data?

Stem	Leaf
0	6 8
1	0 5 5 8
3	2 4 6

range _____

median _____

mode _____

2 Use the data to complete the stem and leaf plot.

Ms. T's Bus Route Trip Times (in minutes)		
25	27	28
30	22	31
32	27	25
28	28	40

Stem	Leaf

3 What is the range of the data?

4 What is the mode of the data?

5 What is the median of the data?

6 How many times did the bus trip take more than a half hour?

Circle the letter for the correct answer.

7 The stem and leaf plot below shows the points scored by the football team so far this season.

Stem	Leaf
0	7 7
1	2 4
2	1 1 1 4 7

Which statement is *not* supported by the information in the stem and leaf plot?

A Most frequently, the team scored 21 pounds

B The team never scored more than 20 points above its lowest score.

C The team won more games than it lost.

D The team has played 9 games so far this season.

8 Which stem and leaf plot accurately represents the data below?

Pecan Tree Height (feet)				
30	22	25	38	47
31	34	35	45	40
32	27	36	32	25

A

Stem	Leaf
2	2 5
3	0 1 2 5 6 8
4	0 5

B

Stem	Leaf
2	2 5 7
3	0 1 2 5 6 8
4	0 5

C

Stem	Leaf
2	2 5 7
3	0 1 2 2 5 6 8
4	0 5 7

D

Stem	Leaf
2	2 5 5 7
3	0 1 2 2 4 5 6 8
4	0 5 7

Unit 33 Mini-Lesson ★
Display and Interpret Data

Standard

V. Probability and Statistics

6.10A (SS) Select and use an appropriate representation for presenting and displaying different graphical representations of the same data including line plot, line graph, bar graph, and stem and leaf plot.

6.10D (RS) Solve problems by collecting, organizing, displaying, and interpreting data.

Model the Skill

◆ **Say:** *Today we are going to look at data and at various ways to display it. We have already made line plots and stem and leaf plots to show data.*

◆ **Say:** *A bar graph lets us compare data easily by looking at the length of each bar.* **Ask:** *What kind of data is best shown on a bar graph?* Discuss discrete data including length, area, height, weight, attendance, votes, etc.

◆ **Ask:** *What kind of data is best shown on a line graph?* Discuss data that shows change over time, including growth rates, temperature, sales, etc.

◆ **Ask:** *If I collect data on the height of a corn plant over 8 weeks, what kind of graph would I most likely use?* (line graph) *How could I best display data on the height of 8 varieties of corn at full growth?* (line plot, stem and leaf, or bar graph) Make up some data points for each scenario and sketch a line graph and a bar graph on the board. Discuss the different displays.

◆ Assign students the appropriate practice page(s) to support their understanding of the skill.

Assess the Skill

Use the following problems to pre-/post-assess students' understanding of the skill.

Have students answer questions about the data in the graph below.

What data does the graph show?

What is the range of the data?

What is the mode of the data?

What is the approximate mean of the data? How can you tell without calculating?

Which animal is taller, the ibis or the egret? How much taller in inches?

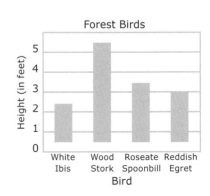

Name _____ Date _____

Complete each graph or plot and answer the questions.

 1

Height of Tomato Plants in the Garden (inches)							
18	23	24	26	32	19	28	19
24	28	31	30	28	32	28	

Stem	Leaf
1	8
2	
3	

2 Which display of the data do you like better? Why?

_____

3 What is the most common height of the tomato plants?

_____

4 What is the range in height of the tomato plants?

_____

5

Students Who Take the Bus to School		
Grade	Number of Boys	Number of Girls
6	130	170
7	145	135
8	180	115

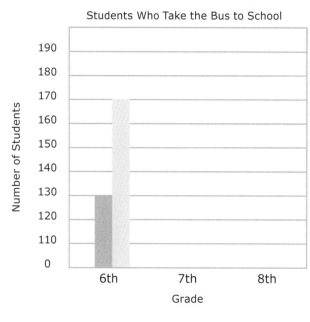

Students Who Take the Bus to School

6 Which grade takes the bus more than any other group?

_____

7 Which grade has the closest ratio of boys and girls riding the bus?

_____

 ☆ **Tell why a double bar graph is a good choice to display the data in Problem 5.**

Name _____ **Date** _____

Make a graph or plot and answer the questions.

1. Which type of graph will best display the data? Choose among bar graph, line plot, or line graph. Explain your choice.

_____

Cost of Car Insurance	
Year	**Annual Cost**
2012	$2,400
2010	$2,000
2008	$2,000
2006	$1,700
2004	$1,350

2. Make a graph to display the data.

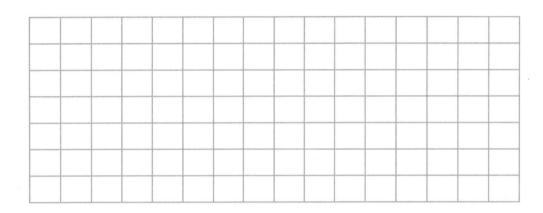

3. Title the graph at right.

_____

4. On which two days is it most likely that it will not rain, sleet, or snow?

5. How much greater is the chance of precipitation on Thursday compared to Wednesday?

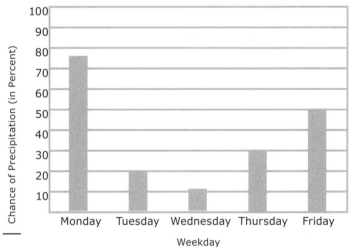

6. In this five-day forecast, how many days show a 50% or greater chance of precipitation?

 Tell how you used the graph to answer Problems 3 and 4.

Name _____ Date _____

Solve.

1 The class voted on favorite ice cream flavors. Twenty-five students voted. Kyle wants to survey at least ten teachers for their favorite flavor. When he completes his survey, how should he display the data? Explain your answer.

_____

_____

2 Ana Laura is writing a science report on the atmosphere and wants to show the different percentage of elements that make up the air that we breathe. How should she display the data? Explain your answer.

_____

_____

Circle the letter for the correct answer.

3 The graph shows the daily high temperature recorded in July in Dallas.

Which statement is *not* supported by the information in the graph?

A The range of temperature in 2000 and 2012 is the same.

B The greatest difference in temperature between 2000 and 2012 for this period is 5 degrees.

C The high temperature stayed the same for 3 days in July 2000.

D The high temperature stayed the same for 3 days in July 2012.

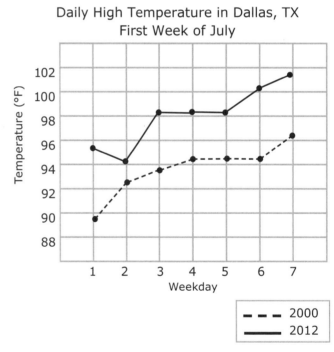

Daily High Temperature in Dallas, TX
First Week of July

2000
2012

4 How many degrees hotter is the hottest day in 2012 than the hottest day in 2000?

A 2°F

B 3°F

C 4°F

D 5°F

Unit 34 Mini-Lesson ★
Display Data in Circle Graphs

Standard

V. Probability and Statistics

6.10C (SS) Sketch circle graphs to display data.

6.12A Communicate mathematical ideas using, language, efficient tools, appropriate units, and graphical, numerical, physical, or algebraic mathematical models.

Model the Skill

◆ **Say:** *Today we are going to learn about a different kind of graph. A circle graph shows the relationship of the parts to the whole. This kind of graph is also known as a pie chart.* **Ask:** *Why do you think it is called that?*

◆ Draw a circle on the board and divide it into 2 sections. Divide one of the sections in half and then half again. Discuss the pieces of "pie" and what they represent: 1/2, 1/4, 1/8.

◆ **Ask:** *If this circle represents the school budget and this part* [the half] *represents the amount spent on books, how much of the budget is spent on books?* (half) *If the budget is $10,000, then how much money will be spent on books?* ($5,000) *If the budget is $500,000, how much will be spent on books?* ($250,000) Have students help make a circle graph for the "school" budget, labeling each section (e.g., football, other sports, library, supplies, technology, repairs)

◆ Create other contexts for the circle graph and ask questions about the relationship of the data. Guide students to write fractions of the whole to represent the data.

◆ Assign students the appropriate practice page(s) to support their understanding of the skill.

Assess the Skill

Use the following problems to pre-/post-assess students' understanding of the skill.

Have students complete a circle graph to represent the data.

Votes for School Colors

Red and White   200

Black and White   50

Blue and White   100

Red and Blue   50

Name _____ Date _____

Use the data to complete each graph.

Fish in a Home Aquarium

Fish	Number
Goldfish	8
Neon Tetra	12
Angel Fish	4

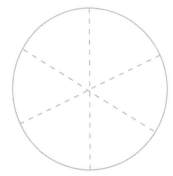

Fish in a Store Aquarium

Fish	Number
Goldfish	60
Angel Fish	40
Catfish	20
Guppies	40

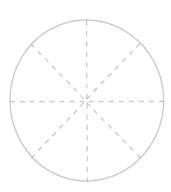

Solve.

3 The graph shows how David spends $100 a week at community college.

How much does David spend on food? _____

What fraction of the total is that? _____

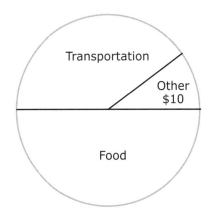

4 What fraction of the budget is NOT spent on transportation or food? _____

5 How much money does David spend on transportation? _____

What fraction of the total is that? _____

 Tell how you sketched the graph for Problem 2.

Name _____ Date _____

Sketch a circle graph for each set of data.

1 The Get Out the Vote Committee surveyed 450 students during the campaign season for the student council.

Survey Results	
Party	Votes
Red	75
Blue	150
Green	225

2 Renee earns $80 each week from delivering papers on her paper route. The table shows how she uses the money.

Renee's Weekly Salary	
Usage	Amount
Bus Fare	$25
Snacks & Misc.	$10
Phone bill	$15
Savings	$30

Solve.

3 The graph shows Rachel's homework for the first week of March.

How many hours of Science homework did Rachel have? _____

What fraction of the total is that? _____

4

What fraction of the time was not spent doing Spanish homework? _____

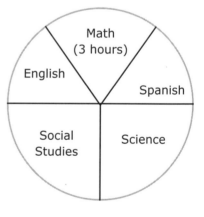

5 How much time did Rachel spend doing Math and Science homework? _____

What fraction of the total is that? _____

 Tell how you found the fractions of the whole that the data in Problem 1 represented.

Name _____ Date _____

Solve.

1 Sketch a circle graph to display the following information.

Weekly TV Sales by Store	
Store	Units Sold
A	135
B	180
C	45

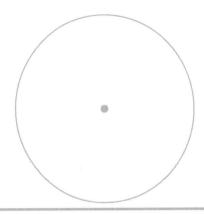

2 What is the total number of TV sales for the week based on the data above?

_____

3 Store C sold the fewest TVs. What fraction of the total weekly sales is that?

_____

4 Explain how you knew what to sketch on the circle graph to represent Store C's sales.

5 What fraction of the total units sold represents the sales made by Stores B and C?

Circle the letter for the correct answer.

6 One thousand students were surveyed about their favorite summer sport. The table below shows the survey results.

Favorite Summer Sport	
Sport	Votes
Swimming	400
Biking	250
Hiking	250
Baseball	100

Which circle graph accurately shows this information?

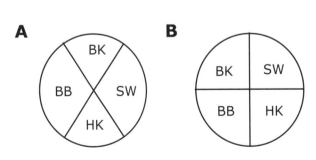

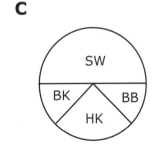

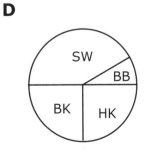

Grade 6 STAAR Mathematics Practice Assessment 1

Name _____ **Date** _____

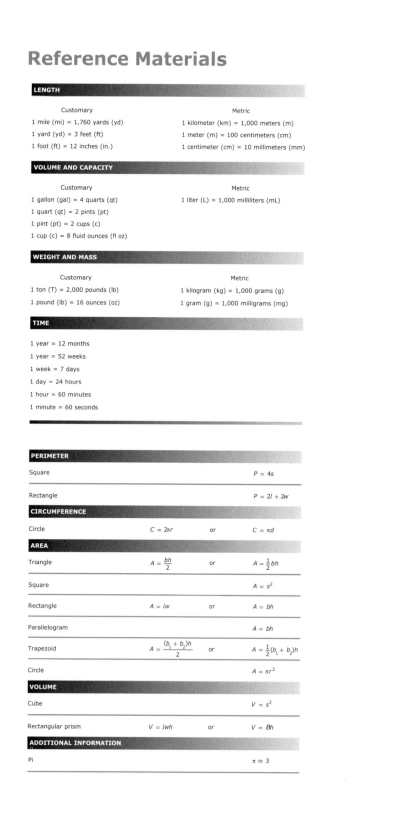

Reference Materials

LENGTH

Customary	Metric
1 mile (mi) = 1,760 yards (yd)	1 kilometer (km) = 1,000 meters (m)
1 yard (yd) = 3 feet (ft)	1 meter (m) = 100 centimeters (cm)
1 foot (ft) = 12 inches (in.)	1 centimeter (cm) = 10 millimeters (mm)

VOLUME AND CAPACITY

Customary	Metric
1 gallon (gal) = 4 quarts (qt)	1 liter (L) = 1,000 milliliters (mL)
1 quart (qt) = 2 pints (pt)	
1 pint (pt) = 2 cups (c)	
1 cup (c) = 8 fluid ounces (fl oz)	

WEIGHT AND MASS

Customary	Metric
1 ton (T) = 2,000 pounds (lb)	1 kilogram (kg) = 1,000 grams (g)
1 pound (lb) = 16 ounces (oz)	1 gram (g) = 1,000 milligrams (mg)

TIME

1 year = 12 months
1 year = 52 weeks
1 week = 7 days
1 day = 24 hours
1 hour = 60 minutes
1 minute = 60 seconds

PERIMETER

Square		$P = 4s$
Rectangle		$P = 2l + 2w$

CIRCUMFERENCE

Circle	$C = 2\pi r$	or	$C = \pi d$

AREA

Triangle	$A = \dfrac{bh}{2}$	or	$A = \frac{1}{2}bh$
Square			$A = s^2$
Rectangle	$A = lw$	or	$A = bh$
Parallelogram			$A = bh$
Trapezoid	$A = \dfrac{(b_1 + b_2)h}{2}$	or	$A = \frac{1}{2}(b_1 + b_2)h$
Circle			$A = \pi r^2$

VOLUME

Cube			$V = s^3$
Rectangular prism	$V = lwh$	or	$V = Bh$

ADDITIONAL INFORMATION

Pi	$\pi \approx 3$

1 Pam took a survey of the students in her class. She asked them how they got to school this morning. The table below shows the results of her survey.

Transportation Survey

Kind of Transportation	Number of Students
Walk	39
Bike	9
Car	24
Bus	48

What decimal represents the fraction of students who rode a bike to school?

A 0.075

B 0.09

C 0.75

D 0.90

2 Samantha is a barista at a local coffee shop. She served three kinds of drinks this morning. The table below shows the drinks she served.

Drinks Served

Drink	Number Served
Coffee	61
Espresso Drink	23
Tea	16

What decimal represents the fraction of the drinks that were espresso drinks?

Record your answer and fill in the bubbles.
Be sure to use correct place value.

3 Kelly conducted a survey among her classmates on number and types of pets. The table below shows the results of her survey.

Pets Survey

Response	Number of Students
Have Only a Cat	7
Have Only a Dog	4
Have a Cat and a Dog	3
Have No Pets	9

What decimal represents the fraction of students in Kelly's class that have pets?

A 0.12

B 0.16

C 0.28

D 0.61

4 Paul is in charge of ordering the food for a large business meeting. The table below shows the meals he ordered for the meeting.

Meals Ordered

Meal	Orders
Grilled Cheese	19
Super Burger	10
Salmon Salad	11

What decimal represents the fraction of people in the meeting who requested the salmon salad?

A 0.11

B 0.275

C 0.51

D 0.725

5 The table below shows the members of the track team of a high school by grade.

Track Team by Grade

Grade	Runners
9th Grade	15
10th Grade	8
11th Grade	7
12th Grade	10

What decimal represents the fraction of members of the track team that are in tenth grade?

A 0.20

B 0.40

C 0.375

D 0.15

---

6 The table below shows the results of a dance competition.

Dance Competition Results

Dancer	Number of Votes
Alissa	24
Grover	18
Roger	51
Marta	27

What decimal represents the fraction of votes that the winner of the dance competition received?

A 0.375

B 0.425

C 0.51

D 0.575

7 Dex is $1\frac{1}{8}$ inches shorter than his sister Mallory. Mallory is $58\frac{3}{4}$ inches tall. How tall is Dex?

A $57\frac{1}{8}$ in.

B $57\frac{1}{4}$ in.

C $57\frac{1}{2}$ in.

D $57\frac{5}{8}$ in.

8 Timothy broke his record jump in the long jump by 1.25 meters. His new record is 8.8 meters. What was his old record?

A 7.35 m

B 7.55 m

C 7.65 m

D 7.75 m

9 The Smith family just had twin babies, Jess and Joss. Jess was born with a length of $20\frac{1}{4}$ inches. Joss was $\frac{3}{8}$ inch longer than his twin. How long was Joss?

A $19\frac{1}{8}$ in.

B $19\frac{3}{4}$ in.

C $19\frac{7}{8}$ in.

D $20\frac{5}{8}$ in.

STAAR Mathematics Practice Grade 6 • ©2013 Newmark Learning, LLC

10 Ruthie is a sculptor. She carved a marble statue that is 3.3 meters high. The statue rests on a marble stand that is 0.25 meters high. How tall are the statue and the stand together?

    A 5.8 m

    B 3.55 m

    C 3.325 m

    D 3.05 m

---

11 Jason competes in the high jump in track. His new record is $62\frac{1}{2}$ inches. This is $3\frac{1}{2}$ better than his previous record. What was his previous record?

    A $59\frac{1}{4}$ in.

    B $60\frac{1}{4}$ in.

    C 59 in.

    D 60 in.

---

12 Frank is signing autographs. He signs about 12 autographs every 10 minutes. There are 67 people in line to get autographs. Which is a good estimate for how long it will take Frank to give everyone an autograph?

    A 60 minutes

    B 75 minutes

    C 85 minutes

    D 90 minutes

---

13 Emily is writing thank-you cards for people who attended her wedding. There were 112 people in attendance. She writes cards at a rate of 15 cards per day. Based on this information, which of the following is a reasonable conclusion?

    A She will have written less than half of the cards after 4 days.

    B She will have written less than a third of the cards after 3 days.

    C She will have written more than 50 cards after 3 days.

    D She will write all thank-you cards within 8 days.

14 Matt took 411 pictures this year and submitted them to the yearbook committee. If they accept 10% of his photos, and the yearbook is 256 pages long, what percentage of the pages of the yearbook could contain Matt's photography?

A 10%

B 1/16

C 16%

D 62%

15 Lanh is transcribing an interview. The interview is 112 minutes long. His transcribing rate is about 23 minutes per hour. Based on this information, which of the following statements is a reasonable conclusion?

A He will have transcribed less than half of the interview after 3 hours.

B He will have transcribed more than half of the interview after 3 hours.

C He will have transcribed more than 60 minutes of the interview after 2 hours.

D He will have transcribed fewer than 40 minutes of the interview after 2 hours.

16 Miguel is editing a batch of 112 photographs. He edits at a rate of 17 photographs per hour. Based on this information, after how many hours will he be at least halfway done?

A 3 hours

B 4 hours

C 5 hours

D 6 hours

17 Stephanie is going to read a 385-page book that she borrowed from the library. She wants to read roughly the same number of pages each day. The book is due in 10 days. Based on this information, how many pages should she try to read each day?

A 40 pages

B 50 pages

C 60 pages

D 65 pages

18 On any given day, 5 out of 7 yogis that come into Mitra Yoga studio are women. On Thursday, there were 26 men that came into the studio. Based on this information, how many people can you expect to have been at Mitra Yoga studio that day?

A 14

B 65

C 91

D 140

19 On any sunny day, Carla expects 3 out of every 5 people to wear sunglasses. On Thursday, it was sunny and there were 68 people at the park. Based on this information, how many people can you expect to have been wearing sunglasses that day?

Record your answer and fill in the bubbles.

Be sure to use the correct place value.

20 At a concert, the band expects that 1 out of every 8 people who attend will buy a T-shirt. If the band sold 24 T-shirts, how many people would you expect to have gone to the concert?

    A 60

    B 80

    C 160

    D 190

21 The chances of getting a prize in a Blue Burst Berry Flakes cereal box is 1 in 5. If there are 74 boxes of cereal at the grocery store, how many prizes can you expect to be in this grocery store?

    A 15

    B 20

    C 25

    D 30

22 Pam runs a lemonade stand. The table below shows how much money she earned, in dollars, based on how many hours she kept the stand open.

Lemonade Stand Earnings

Number of Hours	Earnings (in Dollars)
2	62
3	93
5	155
6	186
h	E

What expression could be used to find E, the earnings Pam would have if she kept the lemonade stand open for h hours?

    A $31h$

    B $31 + h$

    C $62h$

    D $62 + h$

23 Jeffrey's family owns a building. The table below shows how much money he collects, in dollars, based on how many apartment units pay rent.

Rent for the Building

Number of Units	Rent (in Dollars)
2	1,420
3	2,130
5	3,550
a	R

What expression could be used to find R, the amount of rent Jeffrey collects if he collects rent from a apartment units?

A $1{,}420a$

B $1{,}420 + a$

C $710a$

D $710 + a$

---

24 The table below shows the amount of calories Rob eats based on how many servings of potato chips he consumes.

Calories in Potato Chips

Number of Servings	Calories
2	310
3	465
5	775
s	C

What expression could be used to find C, the number of calories Rob consumes if he eats s servings of potato chips?

A $310s$

B $155 + s$

C $155 + 2s$

D $155s$

25 The table below shows the amount of calories Andy burns based on how many miles he runs.

Calories Burned Running

Miles Run	Calories
2	250
3	375
5	625
m	C

What expression could be used to find C, the number of calories Andy burns if he runs m miles?

A 125m

B 125 + m

C 125 + 2m

D 250m

---

26 Colin transcribed 80 minutes of an interview in 5 hours. He transcribed 15 minutes in each of the first 3 hours, and n minutes in the fourth hour. Which equation can be used to find m, the number of minutes of the interview Colin transcribed in the fifth hour?

A $m = 80 - (15 \cdot n)$

B $m = 80 - (15 \cdot n) - 3$

C $m = 80 - 3(15 + n)$

D $m = 80 - (15 \cdot 3) - n$

---

27 Hugo read 320 pages of a book in 7 days. He read 50 pages in each of the first 4 days, and t pages on each of the fifth and sixth days. Which equation can be used to find p, the number of pages of the book Hugo read on the seventh day?

A $p = 320 - (50 \cdot 2t)$

B $p = 320 - (50 \cdot 4) - 2t$

C $p = 320 - (50 \cdot 2) - 4t$

D $p = 320 - (6 \cdot t) - 50$

28 Hannah baked 86 cookies in 4 batches. She baked c cookies in each of the first 2 batches, and 15 cookies in the third batch. Which equation can be used to find b, the number of cookies Hannah baked in the fourth batch of cookies?

A $b = 86 - (15 \cdot 2c)$

B $b = 86 - (2 \cdot c) - 15$

C $b = 86 - 2(15 + c)$

D $b = 86 - (15 \cdot 2) - c$

29 For a census, Ian took surveys of 145 households in 5 days. He surveyed 38 households on each of the first 3 days, and h households on the fourth day. Which equation can be used to find g, the number of households Ian surveyed on the fifth day?

A $g = 145 - (38 \cdot 3) - 5h$

B $g = 145 - (3 \cdot h) - 38$

C $g = 145 - (38 + 3h)$

D $g = 145 - (38 \cdot 3) - h$

30 Which of the following could be the angle measurements for $\triangle DEF$, if $\triangle DEF$ is an acute triangle?

A $m\angle D = 90°, m\angle E = 30°, m\angle F = 60°$

B $m\angle D = 100°, m\angle E = 50°, m\angle F = 30°$

C $m\angle D = 60°, m\angle E = 40°, m\angle F = 80°$

D $m\angle D = 90°, m\angle E = 45°, m\angle F = 45°$

31 Which of the following could be the angle measurements for quadrilateral $CDEF$, if $m\angle C = 30$?

A $m\angle D = 90°, m\angle E = 90°, m\angle F = 150°$

B $m\angle D = 100°, m\angle E = 50°, m\angle F = 130°$

C $m\angle D = 120°, m\angle E = 150°, m\angle F = 90°$

D $m\angle D = 90°, m\angle E = 90°, m\angle F = 90°$

32 The circumference of a circular fountain is 28 feet. Which of the following expressions represents the radius of the fountain?

A $\dfrac{28}{\pi}$

B $28 \cdot \pi$

C $28 \cdot 2\pi$

D $\dfrac{28}{2\pi}$

---

33 The radius of a circular rug is 8 feet. Which of the following expressions represents the circumference of the rug?

A $\dfrac{8}{\pi}$

B $8 \cdot \pi$

C $8 \cdot 2\pi$

D $\dfrac{8}{2\pi}$

---

34 The diameter of a circular garden is 9 feet. Which of the following expressions represents the circumference of the garden?

A $\dfrac{9}{\pi}$ 9

B $9 \cdot \pi$

C $9 \cdot 2\pi$

D $\dfrac{9}{2\pi}$

---

35 The circumference of a circular bird bath is 157 centimeters. What is the radius of the bird bath?

Record your answer and fill in the bubbles.
Be sure to use correct place value.

STAAR Mathematics Practice Grade 6 • ©2013 Newmark Learning, LLC

36 There are 3 vertices of rectangle *ABCD* plotted on the coordinate grid below. The fourth vertex of the rectangle will be point *D*.

Which of the following ordered pairs best represents point *D*?

A $(4\frac{1}{2}, 3)$

B $(7\frac{1}{2}, 3)$

C $(3, 4\frac{1}{2})$

D $(4\frac{1}{2}, 7\frac{1}{2})$

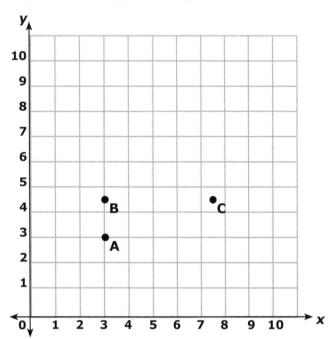

37 There are 3 vertices of rectangle *DEFG* plotted on the coordinate grid below. The fourth vertex of the rectangle will be point *G*.

Which of the following ordered pairs best represents point *G*?

A $(5\frac{1}{2}, 3\frac{1}{2})$

B $(2, 5\frac{1}{2})$

C $(2, 3\frac{1}{2})$

D $(8, 3\frac{1}{2})$

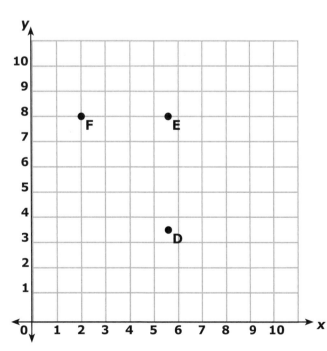

38 The figure below represents the floor of a building. Use a ruler to measure the dimensions of the figure to the nearest ½ inch.

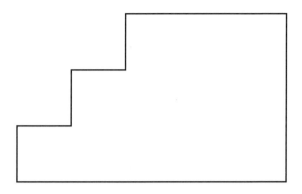

Scale
0.5 in. = 20 ft

Which is closest to the perimeter in feet of the floor of the actual building?

A 140 ft

B 160 ft

C 280 ft

D 320 ft

---

39 The figure below represents the floor of a room. Use a ruler to measure the dimensions of the figure to the nearest ½ inch.

Which is closest to the perimeter in feet of the floor of the room?

A 80 ft

B 90 ft

C 8 ft

D 9 ft

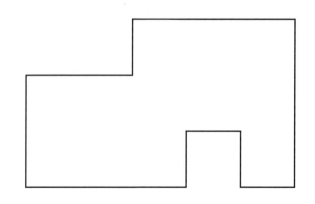

Scale
1.0 in. = 10 ft

40 The figure below represents a garden. Use a ruler to measure the dimensions of the figure to the nearest ½ inch.

Which is closest to the perimeter in feet of the actual garden?

A 96 ft

B 112 ft

C 48 ft

D 56 ft

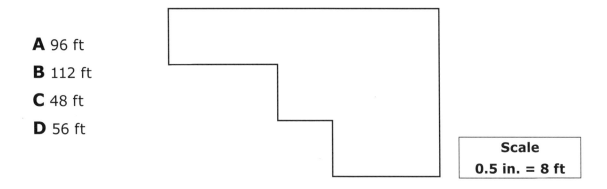

Scale
0.5 in. = 8 ft

---

41 The figure below represents the plan for a porch. Use a ruler to measure the dimensions of the figure to the nearest ½ inch.

Which is closest to the perimeter in feet of actual porch?

Record your answer and fill in the bubbles. Be sure to use the correct place value.

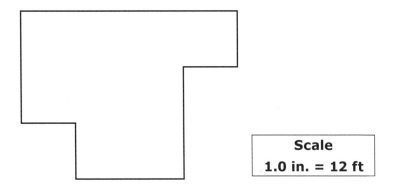

Scale
1.0 in. = 12 ft

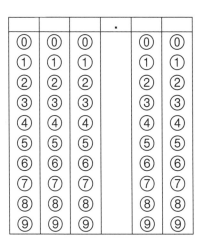

42 Olivia has 3 1/2 gallons of applesauce that she is distributing into 1-pint containers. How many containers can she fill with the applesauce?

    A 28 containers

    B 21 containers

    C 14 containers

    D 7 containers

---

43 George works at a hotel. He pours all the soap he has to fill 1-pint dispensers in each of 40 bathrooms in the hotel. How many gallons did George pour in all?

    A 8

    B 7

    C 6

    D 5

---

44 Amber is a chef who is pouring 4.5 gallons of olive oil into 1-quart containers. How many containers can she fill completely?

    A 16

    B 18

    C 20

    D 27

---

45 Patrick has 22 quarts of apple juice. How much apple juice is this measured in gallons?

    A 4.5

    B 5

    C 5.5

    D 6

STAAR Mathematics Practice Grade 6 • ©2013 Newmark Learning, LLC

46 Rene has 11 kittens. Four of the kittens are gray. The rest are black. If Rene selects a kitten at random, which expression represents the probability that she will select a black kitten?

A 1 – 4/7

B 1 + 4/7

C 1 – 4/11

D 1 – 7/11

47 Ryoko has 9 pairs of shoes. Of the pairs, 6 pairs are athletic. The rest of the shoes are dress shoes. If Ryoko selects a pair of shoes at random, which expression represents the probability that he will select dress shoes?

A 1 – 3/9

B 1 + 3/9

C 1 – 3/15

D 1 – 6/15

48 Debbie has 25 records. Of them, 19 are rock records. The rest are jazz records. If Debbie selects a record at random, which expression represents the probability that she will select a jazz album?

A 1 – 6/19

B 1 + 6/19

C 1 – 6/25

D 1 – 19/25

49 Matthew has 28 books. Of them, 20 are fiction. The rest are nonfiction. If Matthew selects a book at random, which expression represents the probability that he will select a book of nonfiction?

A 1 – 8/20

B 1 – 8/28

C 1 + 8/28

D 1 – 20/28

50 The graph below shows the number of participants in three games at a carnival.

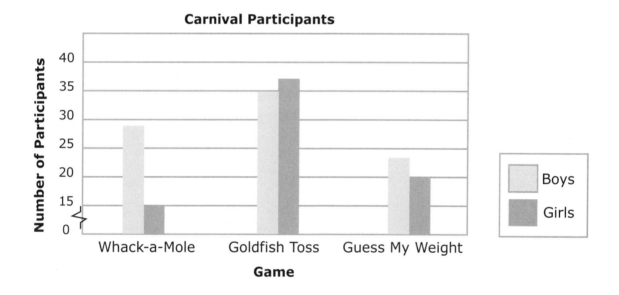

Which statement is NOT supported by the information on the graph?

A Goldfish Toss was the most popular game for girls.

B More boys than girls played every game.

C Goldfish Toss drew approximately 27 more participants than Guess My Weight.

D Whack-a-Mole and Guess My Weight drew about the same number of participants.

51 The graph below shows the number of tickets sold for three movies at a theater.

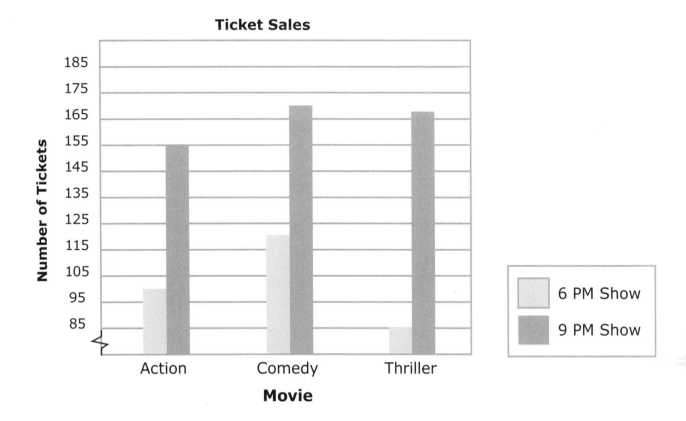

Which statement is NOT supported by the information on the graph?

A The number of tickets sold for 9:00 PM shows is double the number of tickets sold for 6:00 PM shows.

B The number of tickets sold for the 6:00 PM action movie is approximately 18 greater than the number of tickets sold for the 6:00 PM thriller.

C Approximately the same number of tickets were sold for the thriller as the action movie.

D Fifty more tickets were sold for the comedy show at 9:00 PM than the earlier comedy show.

52 The graph below shows the number of students who participated at the track meet on Thursday.

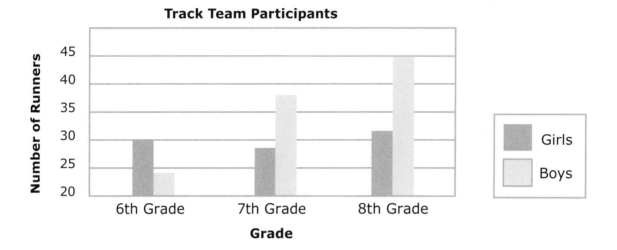

Which statement is NOT supported by the information on the graph?

A The seventh grade has 9 more boys than girls on the team.

B The eighth grade has approximately 22 more runners than the sixth grade has.

C There are more girl runners than boy runners.

D There are more female runners in the eighth grade than in the seventh grade.

Grade 6 STAAR Mathematics Practice Assessment 2

Name _____   **Date** _____

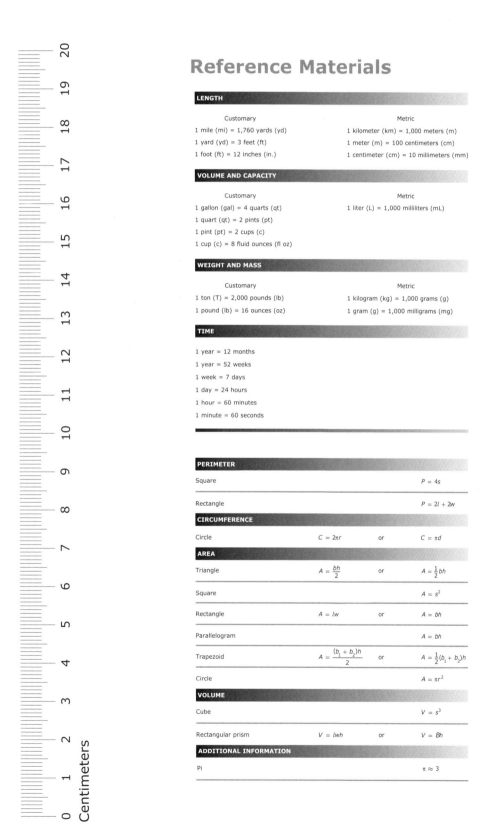

Reference Materials

LENGTH

Customary	Metric
1 mile (mi) = 1,760 yards (yd)	1 kilometer (km) = 1,000 meters (m)
1 yard (yd) = 3 feet (ft)	1 meter (m) = 100 centimeters (cm)
1 foot (ft) = 12 inches (in.)	1 centimeter (cm) = 10 millimeters (mm)

VOLUME AND CAPACITY

Customary	Metric
1 gallon (gal) = 4 quarts (qt)	1 liter (L) = 1,000 milliliters (mL)
1 quart (qt) = 2 pints (pt)	
1 pint (pt) = 2 cups (c)	
1 cup (c) = 8 fluid ounces (fl oz)	

WEIGHT AND MASS

Customary	Metric
1 ton (T) = 2,000 pounds (lb)	1 kilogram (kg) = 1,000 grams (g)
1 pound (lb) = 16 ounces (oz)	1 gram (g) = 1,000 milligrams (mg)

TIME

1 year = 12 months
1 year = 52 weeks
1 week = 7 days
1 day = 24 hours
1 hour = 60 minutes
1 minute = 60 seconds

PERIMETER

Square		$P = 4s$
Rectangle		$P = 2l + 2w$

CIRCUMFERENCE

Circle	$C = 2\pi r$	or	$C = \pi d$

AREA

Triangle	$A = \dfrac{bh}{2}$	or	$A = \frac{1}{2}bh$
Square			$A = s^2$
Rectangle	$A = lw$	or	$A = bh$
Parallelogram			$A = bh$
Trapezoid	$A = \dfrac{(b_1 + b_2)h}{2}$	or	$A = \frac{1}{2}(b_1 + b_2)h$
Circle			$A = \pi r^2$

VOLUME

Cube			$V = s^3$
Rectangular prism	$V = lwh$	or	$V = Bh$

ADDITIONAL INFORMATION

Pi	$\pi \approx 3$

1 The table below shows enrollment in a foreign language program at a community college.

Foreign Language Enrollment

Language	Number of Students
French	90
Russian	45
Japanese	15

What decimal represents the fraction of these students that are enrolled in Russian class?

A 0.30

B 0.40

C 0.45

D 0.60

2 The table below shows the members of a high school choir by grade.

Choir Participants

Grade	Number of Singers
9th Grade	4
10th Grade	10
11th Grade	17
12th Grade	19

What decimal represents the fraction of the choir that is NOT in the twelfth grade?

Record your answer and fill in the bubbles.
Be sure to use correct place value.

3 Rachel is a waitress at a breakfast place. The table below shows the different plates that customers ordered from Rachel on a Wednesday.

Breakfast Orders

Meal	Number Ordered
Eggs Benedict	4
Belgian Waffle	12
Fruit Salad	6
Egg on a Bagel	18

What decimal represents the fraction of customers that ordered the Belgian Waffle?

A 0.52

B 0.30

C 0.28

D 0.11

4 A town has a local singing contest. The table below shows the results of the voting in this contest.

Best Singer Contest Votes

Singer	Number of Votes
Gilligan	45
Ginger	39
Daisy	24
Eric	42

What decimal represents the fraction of votes that the second-place contestant, Eric, received?

A 0.45

B 0.42

C 0.30

D 0.28

5 Reggie is organizing the drinks for a morning meeting at a business conference. The table below shows the final drink order for the group.

Drinks for the Meeting

Drink	Number of Bottles
Apple Juice	12
Orange Juice	10
Water	18

What decimal represents the fraction of meeting participants that ordered water?

A 0.45

B 0.40

C 0.30

D 0.25

---

6 Christie broke her long jump record by 1.15 meters. Her new record is 7.3 meters. What was her previous record?

A 8.45 m

B 8.15 m

C 6.45 m

D 6.15 m

---

7 Kim's length when she was born was $1\frac{1}{2}$ inches less than the length of her sister Karol at birth. Karol was born $18\frac{3}{4}$ inches long. How long was Kim at birth?

A $16\frac{3}{4}$ in.

B $17\frac{1}{4}$ in.

C $19\frac{1}{4}$ in.

D $20\frac{1}{4}$ in.

8 Ashley competes in the shot put in track and field. On her first try, she threw the shot a distance of 18.5 meters. On her next try she threw it 0.75 meters further. What was the length of her second throw?

A 19.25 m

B 20.25 m

C 20.75 m

D 26.0 m

---

9 Teresa bought a set of curtains and hemmed the ends so that they were $1\frac{7}{8}$ inches shorter. Before she hemmed them, they were $63\frac{1}{2}$ inches long. How long were Teresa's curtains after she hemmed them?

A $60\frac{3}{4}$ in.

B $61\frac{3}{8}$ in.

C $61\frac{5}{8}$ in.

D $62\frac{3}{4}$ in.

---

10 Between December and the following July, Briana grew $2\frac{1}{2}$ inches. In December, she was $42\frac{3}{8}$ inches tall. How tall was she in July?

A $45\frac{1}{8}$ in.

B $44\frac{7}{8}$ in.

C $44\frac{4}{8}$ in.

D $45\frac{4}{10}$ in.

11 Lisa is $52\frac{7}{8}$ inches tall. She is wearing a pair of high-heeled shoes that make her $2\frac{1}{2}$ inches taller. How tall is Lisa when she wears this pair of shoes?

A $54\frac{3}{8}$ in.

B $54\frac{3}{10}$ in.

C $55\frac{3}{8}$ in.

D $56\frac{1}{8}$ in.

12 Amy is signing autographs. She can sign about 7 autographs every 5 minutes. There are 48 people in line to get autographs. Which is the best estimate for how long it will take Amy to give each person an autograph?

A 14 minutes

B 35 minutes

C 60 minutes

D 70 minutes

13 Casey wants to read a 318-page book that she borrowed from the library. The book is due 5 days from now. If she wants to read roughly the same number of pages each day, how many pages should she try to read each day?

A 50 pages

B 55 pages

C 60 pages

D 65 pages

14 Justin is transcribing an interview. The interview is 85 minutes long. His transcription rate is about 21 minutes per hour. Based on this information, which of the following statements is a reasonable conclusion?

    A He will have transcribed more than half of the interview after 2 hours.

    B He will have transcribed more than $\frac{1}{3}$ of the interview after an hour.

    C He will have transcribed more than 60 minutes of the interview after 3 hours.

    D He will have transcribed fewer than 40 minutes of the interview after 2 hours.

---

15 Gary is writing thank-you cards for people who came to his fund-raising event. There were 176 people in attendance. He writes cards at a rate of 20 cards per day. Based on this information, which of the following is a reasonable conclusion?

    A He will have written more than half of the cards after 4 days.

    B He will have written more than a third of the cards after 3 days.

    C He will have written more than 120 cards after 5 days.

    D He will have written fewer than 50 cards after 3 days.

---

16 Jeremy is archiving a batch of 147 historical photographs. He archives at a rate of 18 photographs per hour. Based on this information, after how many hours will he be at least halfway done?

    A 3 hours

    B 4 hours

    C 5 hours

    D 6 hours

17 On any given day, 4 out of 6 yogis that come to Sunny's Yoga Studio are women. On Thursday, 126 yogis came to the studio. Based on this information, how many men would you expect to have been at Sunny's Yoga Studio on that day?

A 42

B 21

C 63

D 100

18 At a concert, the band expects that 1 out of every 12 people will buy a CD. If there were 450 people at the concert last night, what is a good estimate for the number of CDs sold by the band?

A 37

B 45

C 54

D 120

19 On a cold day, Richard expects to see 3 out of every 7 people on the train wearing scarves. If there are 63 people on his train car this morning, how many of them does Richard expect to be wearing a scarf?

A 27

B 36

C 45

D 54

20 At an elementary school, 2 out of every 9 children wear eyeglasses. If there are 1,800 students at the school, how many of them can be expected to wear eyeglasses?

Record your answer and fill in the bubbles.
Be sure to use correct place value.

21 Jin runs a car wash. The table below shows how much money he earned, in dollars, based on how many hours he kept the car wash open.

Car Wash Earnings

Number of Hours	Earnings (in Dollars)
2	84
4	168
5	210
h	E

What expression could be used to find E, the earnings Jin would have if he kept the car wash open for h hours?

A 84h

B 84 + h

C 42h

D 42 + h

22 Cathy's family owns a building. The table below shows how much money she collects, in dollars, based on how many apartment units pay rent.

Rent for the Building

Number of Units	Earnings (in Dollars)
2	1,040
3	1,560
5	2,600
a	R

What expression could be used to find R, the amount of rent Cathy collects if she collects rent from a apartment units?

A 520a

B 520 + 2a

C 1,040a

D 1,040 + a

23 The table below shows the amount of calories Amanda eats based on how many servings of jelly beans she consumes.

Calories in Jelly Beans

Number of Servings	Calories
2	82
4	164
5	205
b	C

What expression could be used to find C, the number of calories Amanda consumes if she eats b servings of jelly beans?

A $82b$

B $41 + b$

C $41 + 2b$

D $41b$

---

24 The table below shows the amount of calories Natasha burns based on how many miles she walks.

Calories Burned Walking

Miles Walked	Calories
2	170
4	340
5	425
m	C

What expression could be used to find C, the number of calories Natasha burns if she walks m miles?

A $170m$

B $85m$

C $85 + 2m$

D $85m + 170$

25 Zoe transcribed 115 minutes of an interview in 4 hours. She transcribed n minutes in each of the first 3 hours, and 45 minutes in the last hour. Which equation can be used to find m?

A $m = 115 - (45 \cdot 3n)$

B $m = 115 - (3 \cdot n) - 45$

C $m = 115 - 3(45 + n)$

D $m = 115 - (45 \cdot 3) - n$

---

26 Earl baked 65 cookies in 3 batches. He baked b cookies in each of the first 2 batches. Which equation can be used to find c, the number of cookies in the third batch?

A $c = 65 - 15$

B $c = 65 - (15 \cdot 2)$

C $c = 65 - (2 + b)$

D $c = 65 - (2 \cdot b)$

---

27 Kelly read 415 pages of a book in 5 days. He read 110 pages in each of the first 3 days, and t pages on the fourth day. Which equation can be used to find p, the number of pages Kelly read on the fifth day?

A $p = 415 - (110 \cdot 2) - t$

B $p = 415 - (110 \cdot 3) - t$

C $p = 415 - (110 \cdot 3t)$

D $p = 415 - (6 \cdot t) - 110$

---

28 For a census, Mickey took surveys of 130 households in 6 days. He surveyed 25 households on each of the first 4 days, v households on the fourth day, and $2v$ households on the fifth day. Which equation can be used to find w, the number of households Mickey surveyed on the sixth day?

A $w = 130 - (25 \cdot 4) - 3v$

B $w = 130 - (25 \cdot 4) - 2v$

C $w = 130 - (25 \cdot 4v)$

D $w = 130 - (3 \cdot v) - 25$

29 In $\triangle ABC$, $m\angle A = 30°$. Which kinds of triangle could $\triangle ABC$ be?

    A Obtuse triangle or right triangle

    B Right triangle or equilateral triangle

    C Obtuse triangle or acute triangle

    D Right triangle or acute triangle

30 Which of the following could be the angle measurements for $\triangle DEF$, if $\triangle DEF$ is an obtuse triangle?

    A $m\angle D = 30°$, $m\angle E = 60°$, $m\angle F = 90°$

    B $m\angle D = 60°$, $m\angle E = 60°$, $m\angle F = 60°$

    C $m\angle D = 120°$, $m\angle E = 30°$, $m\angle F = 30°$

    D $m\angle D = 90°$, $m\angle E = 45°$, $m\angle F = 45°$

31 Which of the following could be the angle measurements for quadrilateral $CDEF$, if $m\angle C = 90$?

    A $m\angle D = 85°$, $m\angle E = 90°$, $m\angle F = 95°$

    B $m\angle D = 100°$, $m\angle E = 50°$, $m\angle F = 130°$

    C $m\angle D = 80°$, $m\angle E = 115°$, $m\angle F = 95°$

    D $m\angle D = 100°$, $m\angle E = 90°$, $m\angle F = 110°$

32 The circumference of a circular garden is 40 feet. Which of the following expressions represents the radius of the garden?

    A $\dfrac{40}{\pi}$

    B $40 \cdot \pi$

    C $\dfrac{40}{2\pi}$

    D $40 \cdot 2\pi$

STAAR Mathematics Practice Grade 6 • ©2013 Newmark Learning, LLC

33 The radius of a circular fountain is 13 feet. Which of the following expressions represents the circumference of the fountain?

A $13 \cdot 2\pi$

B $13 \cdot \pi$

C $\dfrac{13}{\pi}$

D $\dfrac{13}{2\pi}$

34 There are 3 vertices of rectangle ABCD plotted on the coordinate grid below. The fourth vertex of the rectangle will be point D.

Which of the following ordered pairs best represents point D?

A $(2\frac{1}{2}, 6)$

B $(6, 5)$

C $(5, 6)$

D $(6, 2\frac{1}{2})$

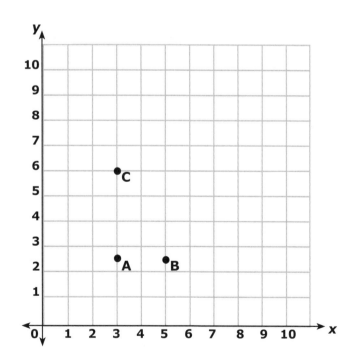

35 There are 3 vertices of rectangle DEFG plotted on the coordinate grid below. The fourth vertex of the rectangle will be point G.

Which of the following ordered pairs best represents point G?

A $(2\frac{1}{2}, 7)$

B $(2, 7\frac{1}{2})$

C $(7\frac{1}{2}, 2)$

D $(7, 2\frac{1}{2})$

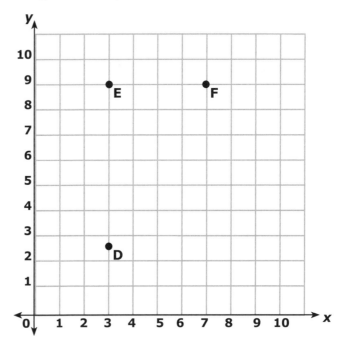

36 There are 3 vertices of rectangle KLMN plotted on the coordinate grid below. The fourth vertex of the rectangle will be point N.

Which of the following ordered pairs best represents point N?

A $(2\frac{1}{2}, 8)$

B $(8, 2\frac{1}{2})$

C $(5, 2\frac{1}{2})$

D $(2\frac{1}{2}, 5)$

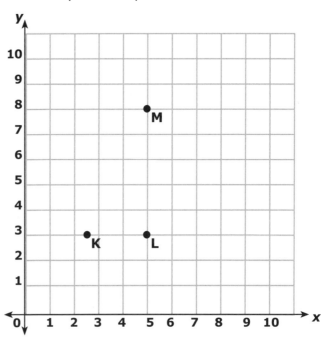

174

37 The figure below represents the floor of a building. Use a ruler to measure the dimensions of the figure to the nearest ½ inch.

Which is closest to the perimeter in feet of the floor of the actual building?

A 216 ft

B 192 ft

C 108 ft

D 81 ft

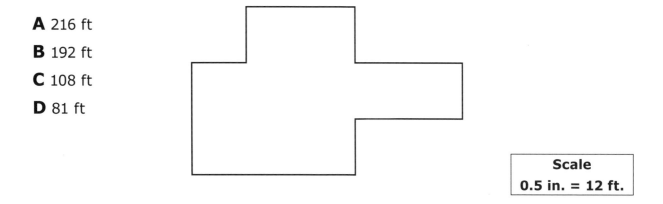

> **Scale**
> **0.5 in. = 12 ft.**

---

38 The figure below represents the plan for a garden. Use a ruler to measure the dimensions of the garden to the nearest ½ inch.

Which is closest to the perimeter in feet of the actual garden?

A 60 ft

B 70 ft

C 240 ft

D 280 ft

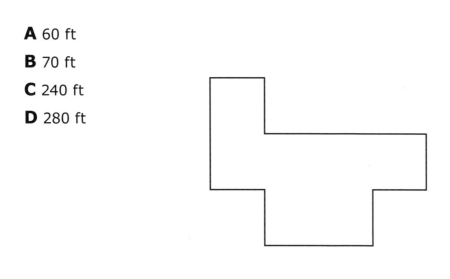

> **Scale**
> **1.0 in. = 40 ft.**

39 The figure below represents the floor of a room. Use a ruler to measure the dimensions of the figure to the nearest ½ inch.

Which is closest to the perimeter in feet of the floor of the actual room?

A 160 ft

B 140 ft

C 80 ft

D 70 ft

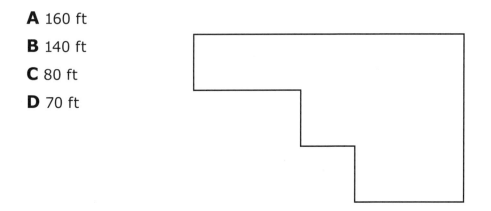

Scale
0.5 in. = 10 ft.

40 The figure below represents the floor of a building. Use a ruler to measure the dimensions of the figure to the nearest ½ inch.

What is closest to the perimeter in feet of the floor of the actual building?

Record your answer and fill in the bubbles.
Be sure to use correct place value.

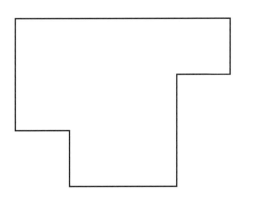

Scale
1.0 in. = 15 ft.

			.		
⓪	⓪	⓪		⓪	⓪
①	①	①		①	①
②	②	②		②	②
③	③	③		③	③
④	④	④		④	④
⑤	⑤	⑤		⑤	⑤
⑥	⑥	⑥		⑥	⑥
⑦	⑦	⑦		⑦	⑦
⑧	⑧	⑧		⑧	⑧
⑨	⑨	⑨		⑨	⑨

41 Meryl has 6.25 gallons of apple juice. How much apple juice is this measured in pints?

    A 25

    B 35

    C 50

    D 75

42 Josh works in a kitchen. He pours all the dish soap he has to fill 1-quart containers. He fills 4.75 gallons. How many containers did Josh fill?

    A 20

    B 19

    C 18

    D 15

43 Ned filled 36 1-pint containers of applesauce. How many gallons of applesauce did he have in all?

Record your answer and fill in the bubbles.

Be sure to use correct place value.

44 Amanda is a chef who is pouring 7.25 gallons of olive oil into 1-quart containers. How many containers can she fill completely?

A 15

B 20

C 29

D 30

45 At the clothing store where Elise works, there are 7 different kinds of sweaters. Of these sweater types, 3 have pockets. If any customer brings a sweater to checkout at random, which expression represents the probability that it will not have pockets?

A 1 + 4/7

B 1 – 4/7

C 1 – 3/11

D 1 – 3/7

46 Sean took 25 photos. Of these photos, 19 were in portrait layout. The rest were in landscape. If Sean chooses a photo at random, which expression represents the probability that it will be in landscape layout?

A 1 + 6/19

B 1 – 6/19

C 1 – 19/25

D 1 – 6/25

47 Ethan has written in 6 notebooks out of the 10 he owns. If Ethan chooses a notebook at random, which expression represents the probability that it will be empty?

A 1 – 6/10

B 1 – 2/6

C 1 – 4/6

D 1 – 4/10

48 Graham works at a bicycle shop, where he recently sold 17 bicycles. Of them, 12 were the men's model bicycles and the rest were women's model bicycles. If Graham chooses a receipt at random from this group of sales, which expression represents the probability that it will be for a women's-model bicycle?

A 1 – 5/17

B 1 – 5/12

C 1 – 12/17

D 1 – 7/12

49 The graph below shows the number of participants in three games at a carnival.

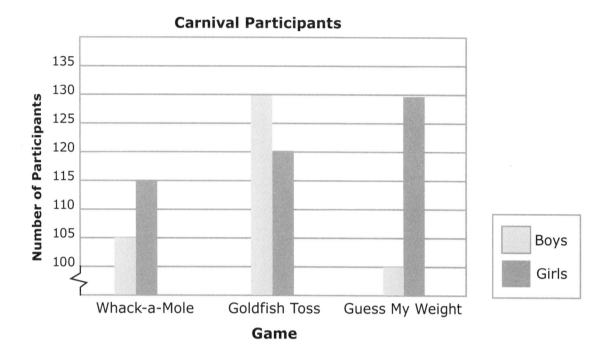

Which statement is NOT supported by the information on the graph?

A The number of girls who played Goldfish Toss is greater than the number of boys who played Whack-a-Mole.

B Approximately 220 children played Whack-a-Mole.

C Goldfish Toss drew approximately 20 more participants than Guess My Weight.

D The number of boys that played Goldfish Toss is approximately 30 more than the number of girls who played Goldfish Toss.

50 The graph below shows the number of students in three grades at a middle school.

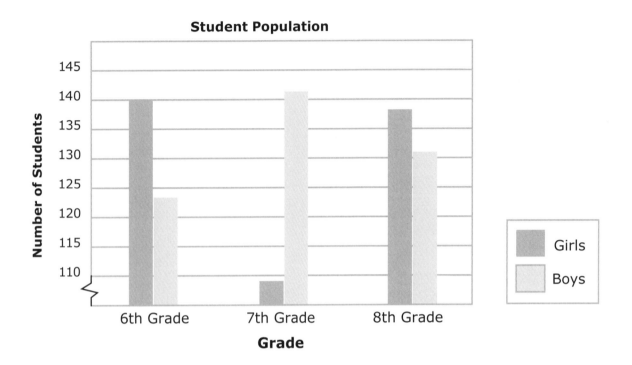

Which statement is NOT supported by the information on the graph?

A The number of girls in sixth grade is greater than the number of boys in seventh grade.

B There are approximately 400 girls that attend the school.

C There are approximately 32 more girls than there are boys in the seventh grade.

D The largest class is the eighth grade class.

51 The graph below shows the number of tickets sold for three movies at a theater.

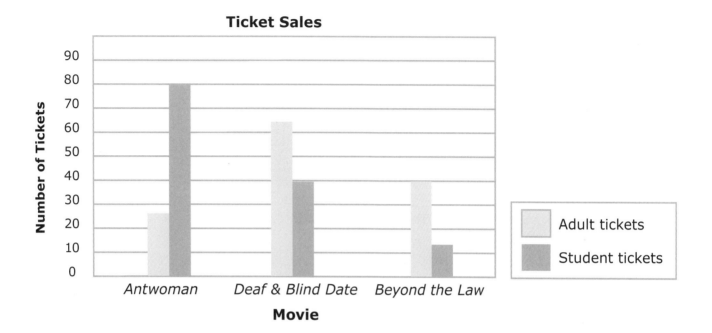

Which statement is NOT supported by the information on the graph?

A There were 5 more adult tickets sold than student tickets.

B More adult tickets were sold for *Deaf & Blind Date* than were sold student tickets for *Antwoman*.

C The number of adult tickets sold for *Beyond the Law* is equal to the number of student tickets sold for *Deaf & Blind Date*.

D More student tickets were sold for *Deaf & Blind Date* than were sold adult tickets for *Antwoman*.

52 The graph below shows the number of runners from each grade on the track team.

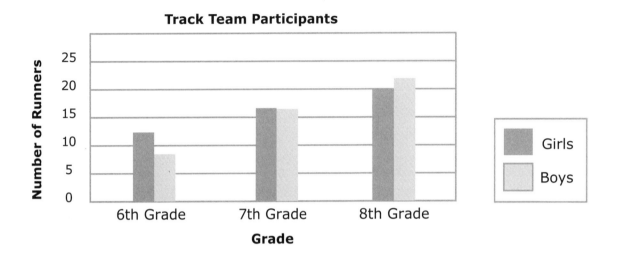

Which statement is NOT supported by the information on the graph?

A The eighth grade has 3 more boys than girls on the team.

B The eighth grade has approximately 22 more runners than the 6th grade has.

C There are more boy runners than girl runners.

D There are more female runners in the 8th grade than in the 7th grade.

Answer Key (Units 1–4)

Unit 1 (p. 5)
1. (1, 3, 9); (1, 2, 3, 4, 6, 12); 3
2. (1, 3, 9); (1, 3, 5, 15); 3
3. (1, 2, 4); (1, 2, 3, 6); 2
4. (1, 2, 3, 6); (1, 2, 5, 10); (1, 2, 4, 7, 14, 28); 2
5. (1, 2, 3, 4, 6, 12); (1, 3, 5, 15); (1, 2, 3, 6, 9, 18); 3
6. (4, 8, 12, 16, 20); (5, 10, 15, 20, 25); 20
7. (4, 8, 12, 16, 20); (10, 20, 30, 40, 50); 20
8. (9, 18, 27, 36, 45); (15, 30, 45, 60, 75); 45
9. (6, 12, 18, 24, 30); (9, 18, 27, 36, 45); 18
10. (8, 16, 24, 32, 40); (12, 24, 36, 48, 60); 24

Unit 1 (p. 6)
1. 5
2. 4
3. 3
4. 12
5. 2
6. 3
7. 10
8. 2
9. 4
10. 63
11. 20
12. 15
13. 12
14. 18
15. 24
16. 24
17. 69
18. 42

Unit 1 (p. 7)
1. Every 24 days
2. 32
3. 17
4. Every 12 days
5. 21
6. 84
7. C
8. A

Unit 2 (p. 9)
1. 1, 2, 3, 6; composite
2. 1, 37; prime
3. 1, 3, 7, 9, 21, 63; composite
4. 1, 2, 4, 7, 14, 28; composite
5. 1, 2, 3, 6, 7, 14, 21, 42; composite
6. 1, 31; prime
7.–10.: Check students' work.
7. 3×2^3
8. $2^2 \times 3$
9. $2^3 \times 5$
10. 3^3

Unit 2 (p. 10)
1.–10.: Check students' work.
1. $2^2 \times 7$
2. 2×3^3
3. 5×3^2
4. $2^2 \times 5$
5. 2×3^2
6. $2^4 \times 3$
7. $2^3 \times 3^2$
8. 2^6
9. $5^2 \times 2$
10. 5^3

Unit 2 (p. 11)
1. Prime, because it is only divisible by 1 and itself
2. $2^2 \times 3 \times 7$
3. 2×31
4. $2^2 \times 5^2$
5. 3, 17; they can't be divided any further
6. 2
7. D
8. C

Unit 3 (p. 13)
1. −4
2. 7
3. 20
4. −5
5. −75
6. 150
7. 4
8. 3; |3|
9. −2; |2|
10. 5; |5|
11. −1; |1|
12. 16; |16|
13. −107; |107|
14. 90; |90|

Unit 3 (p. 14)
1. 50
2. −20
3. −300
4. −16
5. 1,200; −56
6. 500; 6
7. −9; |9|
8. −8; |8|
9. 94; |94|
10. 2; |2|
11. 15; |15|
12. −72; |72|
13. −200; |200|
14. −60; |60|
15. −19; |19|

Unit 3 (p. 15)
1. −10
2. 2,200
3. −8
4. 45
5. 12
6. 674
7. C
8. C

Unit 4 (p. 17)
1. 15
2. 48
3. 8
4. 7
5. 28
6. 7
7. 15
8. 41
9. 35
10. 1
11. 30
12. 9

Unit 4 (p. 18)
1. 17
2. 38
3. 100
4. 1
5. 16
6. 0
7. 1420
8. 33
9. 80
10. 151
11. 93
12. 29.5
13. 48
14. 93
15. 104
16. 144
17. 26
18. 87
19. 78
20. 11

Unit 4 (p. 19)
1. 42 apples
2. 17 pencils
3. 85 cars
4. 41 baseball cards
5. 12 eggs
6. $304
7. B
8. C

Answer Key (Units 5–8)

Unit 5 (p. 21)
1–12 Answers may vary.
1. 40,000   2. 2,000
3. 8,000   4. 20,000
5. 80, 70   6. 100
7. 1,200   8. 900
9. 800   10. 150
11. $600   12. 8 hours
13. No, because 10 x 700 = 7,000, so the answer is not reasonable. It is too low.

Unit 5 (p. 22)
1–8 Answers may vary.
1. 15,000
2. 90,000   3. $50
4. $104,000   5. 55,000
6. 30,000,000
7. 9,000   8. 240
9. 160 years ago
10. 10,000 crepes
11. $120,000   12. 80 years old
13. $6,800   14. 60 miles per hour

Unit 5 (p. 23)
1. $1,250
2. $400
3. $200
4. $600
5. No, because 4,000 x 50 = 200,000. The answer is too low.
6. 40 weeks
7. B
8. B

Unit 6 (p. 25)
1. 267 R1   2. 651 3/7
3. 575   4. 1,682 1/5
5. 304   6. 319.7
7. 57 2/3   8. 850 1/4
9. 106.25   10. 67.25
11. 79.2   12. 411.5
13. 12.8   14. 23
15. 15.05   16. 18.5

Unit 6 (p. 26)
1. 85 6/10   2. 58
3. 68 1/4   4. 52 1/3
5. 12 4/5   6. 56 2/5
7. 1,746   8. 678 1/2
9. 31.25   10. 95.38
11. 191.25   12. 19.88
13. 471.5   14. 553
15. 69.3   16. 18.75

Unit 6 (p. 27)
1. $14.25   2. 42
3. 63   4. 0.23 ft
5. 11   6. 36
7. D   8. B

Unit 7 (p. 29)
1. 1.96   2. 1.05
3. 3.099   4. 0.598
5. 4.46   6. 0.5
7. 0.129   8. 3.837
9. 3.46   10. 2.10
11. 2.34   12. 5.10
13. 1.09   14. 2.12
15. 3.472   16. 4.597

Unit 7 (p. 30)
1. 1.27   2. 1.02   3. 2.3
4. 1.181   5. 2.9   6. 3.74
7. 2.195   8. 1.43   9. 1.62
10. 2.07   11. 2.36   12. 2.848
13. 0.16   14. 0.16   15. 1.33
16. 0.97   17. 5.83   18. 1.33
19. 0.96   20. 0.25   21. 6.155
22. 3.30   23. 0.065 24. 1.571

Unit 7 (p. 31)
1. $56.50
2. $1.49
3. $22.24
4. 8.15 ounces
5. $27.75
6. 3.5 miles
7. D
8. C

Unit 8 (p. 33)
1. 0.5   2. 0.2
3. 0.125   4. 0.375
5. 0.7   6. 0.167
7. 9/10   8. 2/5
9. 7/25   10. 3/20
11. 3/4   12. 1 3/10
13. <   14. <
15. = 16. >
17. = 18. >

Unit 8 (p. 34)
1. 0.375   2. 0.0625
3. 0.8   4. 0.67
5. 0.3   6. 0.583
7. 3/10   8. 1/3
9. 13/50   10. 2 1/4
11. 1 3/8   12. 5/8
13. <   14. >   15. <
16. >   17. >   18. <
19. 1/20, 0.25, 3/5
20. 0.45, 6/8, 12/12

Unit 8 (p. 35)
1. 2/5
2. 13/20
3. 0.625
4. 3.83
5. 1 3/8
6. 52/125
7. C
8. D

STAAR Mathematics Practice Grade 6 • ©2013 Newmark Learning, LLC

Answer Key (Units 9–12)

Unit 9 (p. 37)
1. –1   2. –8
3. 151 and –151
4. 27 and –27
5. <   6. >   7. >
8. >   9. <   10. >
11. >   12. <   13. <
14. >   15. <   16. >
17. >   18. <
19. >   20. <

Unit 9 (p. 38)
1. –7   2. 8   3. –16
4. –252, 252   5. 58
6. –9   7. –14, 14
8. –84, 849. <
10. >   11. <   12. >
13. <   14. <   15. <
16. <   17. >   18. >
19. >   20. >   21. >
22. <   23. <   24. >

Unit 9 (p. 39)
1. A
2. –7, –2, 4, 5
3. C
4. 12, 10, –14, –20
5. B
6. –143, –118, –36, 60, 125
7. B
8. A

Unit 10 (p. 41)
1. 5/6
2. 3/4
3. 1 1/4
4. 1 1/3
5. 1
6. 2/3
7. 1 1/8
8. 7/8

Unit 10 (p. 42)
1. 1/2, <   2. 1 1/4, >
3. 7/10, <   4. 5/8, <
5. 7/9, <   6. 9/10, <
7. 5/8, <   8. 1 3/8, >
9. 32/35, <
10. 11/12, <
11. 13/15, <
12. 5/6, <
13. 1 1/10, >
14. 13/24, <
15. 19/21, <
16. 39/40, <

Unit 14 (p. 43)
1. 7/8
2. 13/20
3. 1 1/35
4. 5 pages
5. 3/8
6. 9 sections
7. D
8. A

Unit 11 (p. 45)
1. 1/6
2. 1/4
3. 3/10
4. 1/3
5. 0
6. 1/6
7. 5/8
8. 1/8

Unit 11 (p. 46)
1. 1/6   2. 1/4
3. 1/2   4. 3/8
5. 5/9   6. 0
7. 3/8   8. 1/8
9. 18/35   10. 1/4
11. 7/15   12. 1/15
13. 3/10   14. 11/24
15. 3/14   16. 31/40

Unit 11 (p. 47)
1. 2/5
2. 9/20
3. 17/40
4. 2/5
5. 6 slices
6. 3 sections
7. A
8. B

Unit 12 (p. 49)
1. 5:15   2. 6:5   3. 5:4
4. 4:6   5. 3:8   6. 3:5
7. 1:3   8. 1:5   9. 1:2
10. 6:8   11. 8:9   12. 2:3
13. 1:5   14. 3:4
15. 10:16   16. 4:6
17. 3:5   18. 5:6

Unit 12 (p. 50)
1. 7:6, 6:7, 1:26
2. 10:3, 3:5, 1:2
3. 1:3, 3:55, 1:55
4. 11:10, 10:11, 1:21
5. 6, 8; 20, 40, 50; 1:5
6. 4, 8; 12, 18; 2:3
7. 1:3   8. 1:5   9. 7:8
10. 1:2   11. 2:3   12. 1:2
13. 1:3   14. 2:3   15. 4:5
16. 3:4   17. 3:4   18. 20:21

Unit 12 (p. 51)
1. 2:3   2. 1:1   3. 2:3
4. 1:5   5. 2:3   6. 1:4
7. C   8. D

Answer Key (Units 13–16)

Unit 13 (p. 53)
1. 25, 2; 25:1; 25 km
2. 1 for $6
3. 1:20   4. 1:$9.20
5. 1:60   6. 1:2
7. 1:30   8. 1:8
9. 1 for $5   10. 1:60
11. 1 for $0.10   12. 1:6
13. 100 mi   14. 120 km
15. 320 km   16. 10 hr
17. 1 hr   18. 2 hr
19. 105 mph   20. 20 kph
21. 10 m/sec

Unit 13 (p. 54)
1. 4:1 2. 1:8 3. 2:1
4. 6/1 5. 4/1 6. 7/1
7. 1:$11.33 8. 3:1
9. 1:$0.40   10. 440 mi
11. 120 mi   12. 150 km
13. 6 hr   14. 20 hr
15. 5 hr   16. 50 mph
17. 5 kph   18. 2 m/sec
19. 1 mi/min or 60 mph
20. 17 km/min or 1,020 kph
21. 40 m/min or 2,400 m/hr

Unit 13 (p. 55)
1. 5 for $1.00; 20 cents
2. 10 for $3.00; 30 cents
3. dozen for $7.00
4. supermarket
5. 100 hr
6. 50 cars/hr
7. B
8. D

Unit 14 (p. 57)
1. 42%   2. 1%
3. 30%   4. 75%
5. 36%   6. 0.5; 50%
7. 0.65; 65%
8. 0.03; 3%
9. 0.08; 8%
10. 0.5; 50%
11. 0.12; 12%
12. 0.05; 5%
13. 0.42; 42%
14. 0.01; 1%
15. 0.07; 7%
16. 0.58; 58%
17. 0.23; 23%

18. 0.09; 9%
19. 0.15; 15%
20. 0.04; 4%
21. 0.75; 75%

Unit 14 (p. 58)
1. 0.59   2. 0.04
3. 0.36   4. 0.60
5. 0.25   6. 0.50
7. 0.25; 25%
8. 0.60; 60%
9. 0.30; 30%
10. 0.50; 50%
11. 7/10; 70%
12. 20/100; 20%
13. 8/100; 8%

14. 65/100; 65%
15. 50/100; 0.50
16. 90/100; 0.90
17. 2/100; 0.02
18. 100/100; 1.00

Unit 14 (p. 59)
1. 65%
2. 80%
3. 20%
4. 25%
5. 60%
6. 40%
7. B
8. C

Unit 15 (p. 61)
1. $2s$ 2. $s + 2$
3. $s - 2$ 4. $s/2$
5. $n + 6$ 6. $n/10$
7. add 1; $x + 1 = y$
8. multiply by 2; $2x = y$
9. multiply by $15; $15s = y$
10. divide by 12; $n/12 = y$

Unit 15 (p. 62)
1. a 2. $8n$
3. a number multiplied by 7; v
4. n; $n/2$
5. a number plus 1, times 4; y
6. n; $n - 3$
7. a number plus 10, divided by 6; n
8. n; $n^2 + 1$
9. divide input by 3; $y = x/3$
10. input squared + 1; $y = x^2 + 1$

11. multiply number of rides by $2.50; $y = \$2.50r$
12. divide number of quarts by 4; $y = n/4$

Unit 15 (p. 63)
1. 3, 7, 8   2. 60 feet
3. 2,116 square yards
4. 19,044 square feet
5. answers may vary, but may include P = 3 ($s^2/s \times 4$)
6. 156 feet
7. A

Unit 16 (p. 65)
1. $y = x + 7$; $x = y - 7$
2. $y = x - 4$; $x = y + 4$
3. $y = x/5$; $x = 5y$
4. $w = 8g$; $g = w/8$
5. $s = p/6$; $p = 6s$

Unit 16 (p. 66)
1. $y = x + 15$; $x = y - 15$
2. $a = b + 5$; $b = a - 5$
3. $r = 7s$; $s = r/7$
4. $A = s^2$; $s = A/s$
5. $4r = p$ or $r = p/4$
6. $s = 20w$ or $w = s/20$

Unit 16 (p. 67)
1. $p = 3s$
2. $s = p/3$
3. $m = 3/4 \times p$ or $(p \times 3) \div 4$
4. D
5. C

STAAR Mathematics Practice Grade 6 • ©2013 Newmark Learning, LLC

Answer Key (Units 17–19)

Unit 17 (p. 69)
1. $n \div 3 = 6$
2. $n + 2 = 16$
3. $y = 2x$
4. $a = c/2$
5. $n + 8 = 32$
6. $b - 4 = n$
7. $p + 3 = 31$
8. $8p = 14$
9. $y = x + 2$
10. $y = 7x$

Unit 17 (p. 70)
1. $n \div 7 = 3$
2. $y = x + 5$
3. $s = t/2$
4. $(a + 8) 2 = b$
5. $2g = 10$
6. $x^2 + 2 = y$
7. $s - 5 = 47; s = 52$
8. $8p = \$17.60; p = \$2.20/lb$
9. $y = x + 4$
10. $w = 21h$

Unit 17 (p. 71)
1. $m = n/3 + 2$
2. $c = 4b$
3. $2h = m$
4. $t/9 = g$
5. $(w \times 3) + 2 = m$
6. B
7. C

Unit 18 (p. 73)
1. right
2. obtuse
3. acute
4. obtuse
5. acute
6. right
7. right
8. acute
9. acute
10. right
11. 50°

Unit 18 (p. 74)
1. obtuse
2. right
3. acute
4. obtuse
5. acute
6. right
7. 180°
8. 60°
9. 30°
10. 60°
11. true
12. obtuse or greatest

Unit 18 (p. 75)
1. B, because all three angles are less than 90°
2. C, because it is a right triangle, which means no angle is greater than 90°
3. 110°
4. 25°
5. 76°
6. M = 50°
7. D
8. A

Unit 19 (p. 77)
1. C
2. A
3. E
4. B
5. 90°
6. 95°
7. 116°
8. 70°

Unit 19 (p. 78)
1. square
2. rectangle
3. trapezoid
4. parallelogram
5. rhombus
6. quadrilateral
7. A
8. A, B, D, E
9. A, B, D, E
10. A, B
11. 120°
12. 58°
13. 45°
14. 55°

Unit 19 (p. 79)
1. squares, rectangles, because they have right angles
2. squares, rectangles, parallelograms,
3. rectangle, rhombus
4. square, rhombus
5. 57°
6. 240°
7. B
8. B

Answer Key (Units 20–24)

Unit 20 (p. 81)
1. AF   2. O
3. radius
4. EO; AO; OF
5. chord
6. 10 meters
7. 9 meters
8. 6 inches
9. yes, because the diameter would be 6 inches, and if $C = \Pi D$, and $\Pi = 3.14$, then 6 x 3.14 is about 18 inches

Unit 20 (p. 82)
1. diameter   2. center
3. chord   4. radius
5. arc   6. radius
7. true
8. true
9. false
10. 325 cm
11. 11 inches
12. $C = d$ x 3.14

Unit 20 (p. 83)
1. 8 meters
2. 6 inches
3. 20.5 meters
4. 23.55 meters
5. B
6. C

Unit 21 (p. 85)
Check students' work.

Unit 21 (p. 86)
1.–6. Check students' work.
7. trapezoid
8.–10. Check students' work.

Unit 21 (p. 87)
1.–4. Check students' work.
5. B
6. C

Unit 22 (p. 89)
1. 70°   2. 110°
3. 180°   4. 130°
5. 50°   6. 90°
7. 160°   8. 30°

Unit 22 (p. 90)
Check students' work.

Unit 22 (p. 91)
1. CDE
2. Check students' work.
3. 30°
4. 60°
5. B
6. D

Unit 23 (p. 93)
1. 500 cm   2. 8 m
3. 3.5 m   4. 6,000 m
5. 1.75 kg   6. 4,300 g
7. 2,250 mL   8. 5 L
9. 5 yd   10. 60 in.
11. 3,520 yd   12. 4 lb.
13. 6,000 lbs. 14. 10 c
15. 2 1/2 gal   16. 12 c

Unit 23 (p. 94)
1. 6,000 cm   2. 72,000 m
3. 45 m   4. 250,000 mg
5. 5,800 m   6. 0.75 L
7. 87,000 mL   8. 400,800 cm
9. 18.9 km   10. 6.125 km
11. 12,320 yd   12. 4.2 t
13. 768 oz   14. 65 yd
15. 540 in.   16. 251 yd
17. 21 gal   18. 128 pt
19. 3.5 kg   20. 8,800 yd

Unit 23 (p. 95)
1. 1 qt
2. 58,000 m
3. no
4. 4,000
5. 3 inches
6. 0.5 L
7. C
8. B

Unit 24 (p. 97)
1. 42 minutes
2. 4.12 kg
3. 20 oz
4. 4 lbs. 3 oz
5. 9 in.
6. 8°C
7. 20 km
8. 5 days
9. 17°
10. 76°

Unit 24 (p. 98)
1. 180 min
2. 83,000 yd
3. 4.25 t
4. 5 lbs. 4 oz
5. 45 in.
6. 28°C
7. 1,200 m
8. 3 hours
9. 115.8 ounces
10. 5 5/8 lbs.

Unit 24 (p. 99)
1. 4:10 P.M.; 7 hours 35 minutes
2. 15 gallons
3. 6.2 hours
4. 50 cm
5. 17°
6. 7 lbs.
7. D
8. A

STAAR Mathematics Practice Grade 6 • ©2013 Newmark Learning, LLC

Answer Key (Units 25–27)

Unit 25 (p. 101)
1. 60; 60; 240 cm
2. 5, 3, 6; 14 m
3. 12, 19; 62 ft
4. c = ~150 cm
5. c = ~15 ft

Unit 25 (p. 102)
Answers may vary.
1. ~41 m
2. ~120 m
3. ~225 m
4. ~ 360 m
5. ~ 60 ft
6. ~800 m
7. ~280 cm
8. ~90 yd

Unit 25 (p. 103)
1. 13 ft
2. 33 cm
3. 80 ft
4. D
5. A

Unit 26 (p. 105)
1. 600 ft^2
2. 12.5 cm^2
3. 18 m^2
4. 400 cm^2
5. 6 m^2
6. 750 ft^2

Unit 26 (p. 106)
1. 25 m^2
2. 12 m^2
3. 28 m^2
4. 21 m^2
5. 77 in^2
6. 81 cm^2
7. 24 m^2
8. 70 ft^2
9. 21 yd^2
10. 80 km^2

Unit 26 (p. 107)
1. 168 ft^2
2. 16.7 yd^2
3. 13.5 cm^2
4. 15 yd^2
5. 3,000 in.^{2}
6. 1,260 cm^2
7. A
8. C

Unit 27 (p. 109)
1. 108 units^3
2. 75.6 in^3
3. 70 ft^3
4. 28 cm^3
5. 97.5 m^3
6. 166.375 in^3
7. 232.8 ft^3
8. 421.875 in^3
9. 181.5 ft^3

Unit 27 (p. 110)
1. 55.69 m^3
2. 34.33 in^3
3. 86.33 ft^3
4. 91.46 in^3
5. 140 in^3
6. 75.6 in^3
7. 43.56 cm^3
8. 107.6 m^3
9. 12.17 ft^3
10. 270.51 cm^3
11. 1,423.83 in^3
12. 98 ft^3

Unit 27 (p. 111)
1. 4 1/4 ft^3
2. 63 ft^3
3. 561 1/8 in^3
4. 0.5 m^3
5. 240,000 mL
6. 205 m^3
7. D
8. C

Answer Key (Units 28–31)

Unit 28 (p. 113)
Check students' work.
1. A or B
2. 1, 2, 3, or 4
3. A1, A2, A3, A4, B1, B2, B3, B4
4. 8
5. 4
6. 6

Unit 28 (p. 114)
Check students' work.
1. 1, 2, 3, 4, 5, 6
2. A, B, C
3. 1A, 1B, 1C, 2A, 2B, 2C, 3A, 3B, 3C, 4A, 4B, 4C, 5A, 5B, 5C, 6A, 6B, 6C
4. make a tree diagram
5. 36   6. 9   7. 8

Unit 28 (p. 115)
1.–2. Check students' work.
3. B
4. B

Unit 29 (p. 117)
Check students' work.
1. square, triangle, circle, or diamond
2. 4
3. 1/4   4. 1/4
5. 3/4   6. 1/6
7. 1/6   8. 5/6
9. 3/6 or 1/2
10. 3/6 or 1/2
11. 2/6 or 1/3

Unit 29 (p. 118)
Check students' work.
1. 1/12
2. 6/12 or 1/2
3. 6/12 or 1/2
4. 4/12 or 1/3
5. 3/12 or 1/4
6. 4/12 or 1/3
7. 9/12 or 3/4
8. 10/12 or 5/6
9. 7 are jelly; 13 are not jelly
10. 1/6   11. 3/6 or 1/2
12. 1/4   13. 3/4

Unit 29 (p. 119)
Check students' work.
1. 1
2. 1/8
3. 4/8 or 1/2
4. 2/8 or 1/4
5. D   6. B

Unit 30 (p. 121)
1. $37; $35   2. 1; 0.75
3. 19.1; 19.5 4. 21; 22
5. 88; 89   6. 2.3; 2
7. 19
8. 3.75, 4.25
9. $27; $26; $25
10. $216.33; $209; none

Unit 30 (p. 122)
1. 79; 80; none
2. 93; 92; 92
3. 84; 85; none
4. 89; 88; 88
5. 1; 0.5; 0.25
6. 94.75; 95.5; 96
7. 8.7; 8.5; 8 8. 3; 3; 2.5
9. 33.4; 34; none
10. 1.75; 1, none

Unit 30 (p. 123)
1. 84.5   2. 40
3. 40 minutes 4. 98
5. 18   6. 1.1
7. B   8. C

Unit 31 (p. 125)
Check students' work.
1. 15
2. 5
3. 1
4. 1
5. Check students' work.
6. 3
7. 2
8. 15 9. 2

Unit 31 (p. 126)
Check students' work.
1. 6   2. 10   3. 10
4. the mode; it shows most students spend 10 hours studying each week
5. 2   6. 2   7. 3
8. 5   9. 2.5
10. the mode; it shows the greatest number of students study 2 hours a night

Unit 31 (p. 127)
Check students' work.
1. 6   2. 83
3. 84
4. 4
5. 3, 4, and 5
6. 4
7. C   8. A

STAAR Mathematics Practice Grade 6 • ©2013 Newmark Learning, LLC

Answer Key (Units 32–34)

Unit 32 (p. 129)
1. Check students' work.
2. 15
3. No, they scored above and below 22 points an even number of times.
4. Check students' work.
5. 11
6. 220
7. the top sales
8. 20

Unit 32 (p. 130)
1. Check students' work.
2. 13
3. 30
4. 85
5. 6
6. 7
7. Check students' work.
8. 20
9. 12
10. 5
11. 18

Unit 32 (p. 131)
1.–6. Check students' work.
1. 30; 15; 15
2. Check students' work.
3. 18
4. 28
5. 28
6. 3
7. C
8. D

Unit 33 (p. 133)
1. Check students' work.
2. Answers may vary.
3. 28
4. 14
5. Check students' work.
6. Grade 6
7. Grade 7

Unit 33 (p. 134)
1. Answers may vary, with line graph or bar graph being acceptable.
2. Check students' work.
3. Answers may vary.
4. Tuesday and Wednesday
5. 20% more likely
6. 2 days (Monday and Friday)

Unit 33 (p. 135)
1. Answers may vary, with double bar graph being the best answer.
2. Answers may vary, with circle graph being the best answer.
3. B
4. D

Unit 34 (p. 137)
1. Check students' work.
2. Check students' work.
3. $50 or 50%; 1/2
4. 1/10
5. $40; 4/10

Unit 34 (p. 138)
1. Check students' work.
2. Check students' work.
3. 4.5 hours; 1/4
4. 5/6
5. 7.5 hours; 5/12

Unit 34 (p. 139)
1. Check students' work.
2. 360
3. 1/8
4. Answers may vary.
5. 5/8
6. D

Answer Key (Practice Tests 1–2)

STAAR
Practice Test 1
pages 141–160

1. A
2. 0.23
3. D
4. B
5. A
6. B
7. D
8. B
9. D
10. B
11. C
12. A
13. D
14. C
15. B
16. B
17. A
18. C
19. 41
20. D
21. A
22. A
23. C
24. D
25. A
26. D
27. B
28. B
29. D
30. C
31. A
32. D
33. C
34. B
35. 25
36. B
37. C
38. D
39. B
40. A
41. 84
42. A
43. D
44. B
45. C
46. C
47. A
48. D
49. B
50. B
51. A
52. C

STAAR
Practice Test 2
pages 162–182

1. A
2. 0.62
3. B
4. D
5. D
6. D
7. B
8. A
9. C
10. B
11. C
12. B
13. D
14. C
15. B
16. C
17. A
18. A
19. A
20. 400
21. C
22. A
23. D
24. B
25. B
26. D
27. B
28. A
29. C
30. C
31. A
32. C
33. A
34. C
35. D
36. A
37. B
38. D
39. A
40. 105
41. C
42. B
43. 4.5
44. C
45. B
46. C
47. A
48. C
49. D
50. A
51. B
52. C

STAAR Mathematics Practice Grade 6 • ©2013 Newmark Learning, LLC